Diana Al-Hadid

unbecoming

Diana
Al-Hadid

unbecoming

Published on the occasion of *unbecoming*
June 7–December 14, 2025
Eli and Edythe Broad Art Museum at Michigan State University

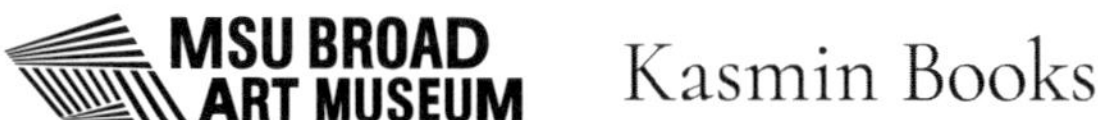

Kasmin Books

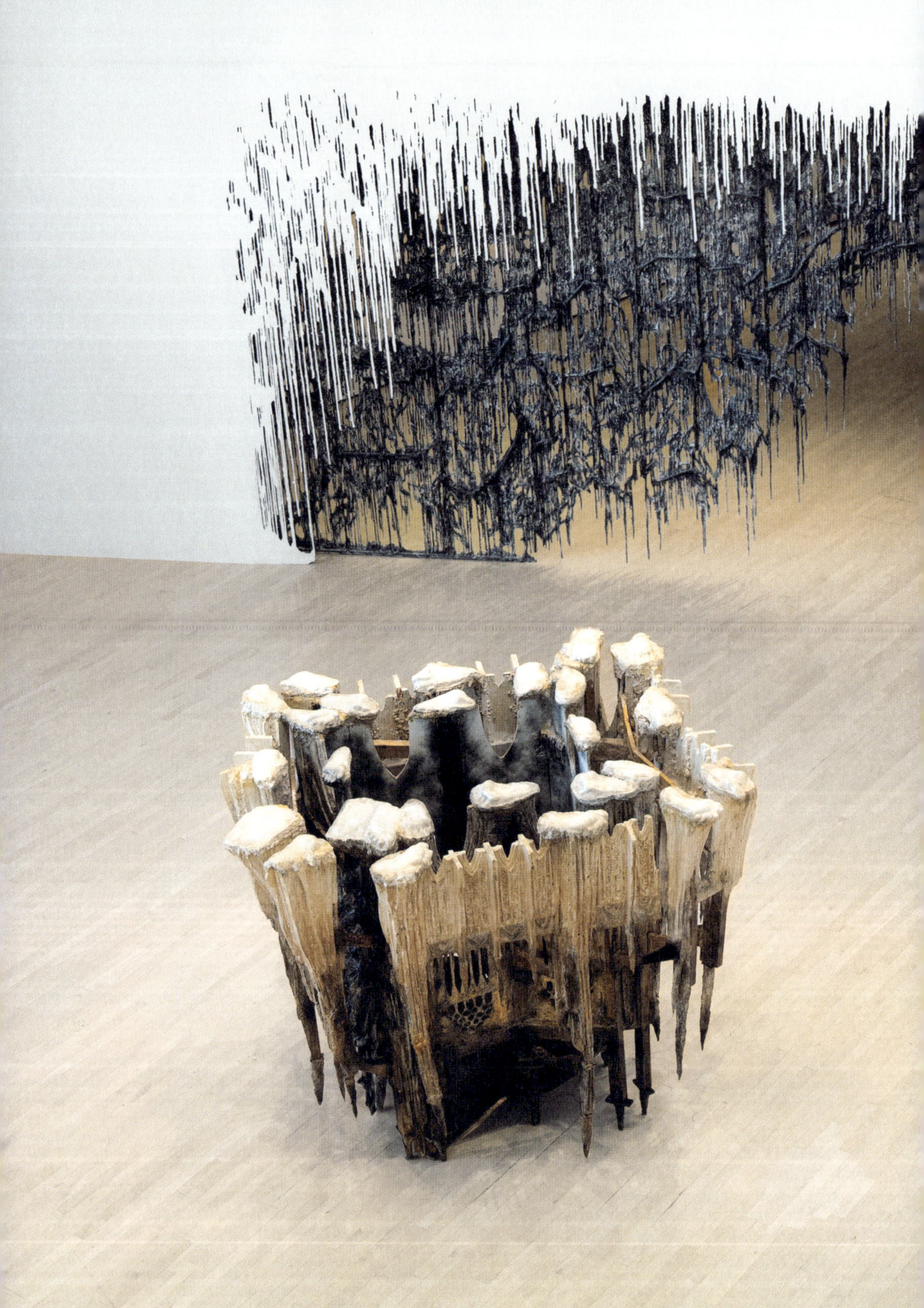

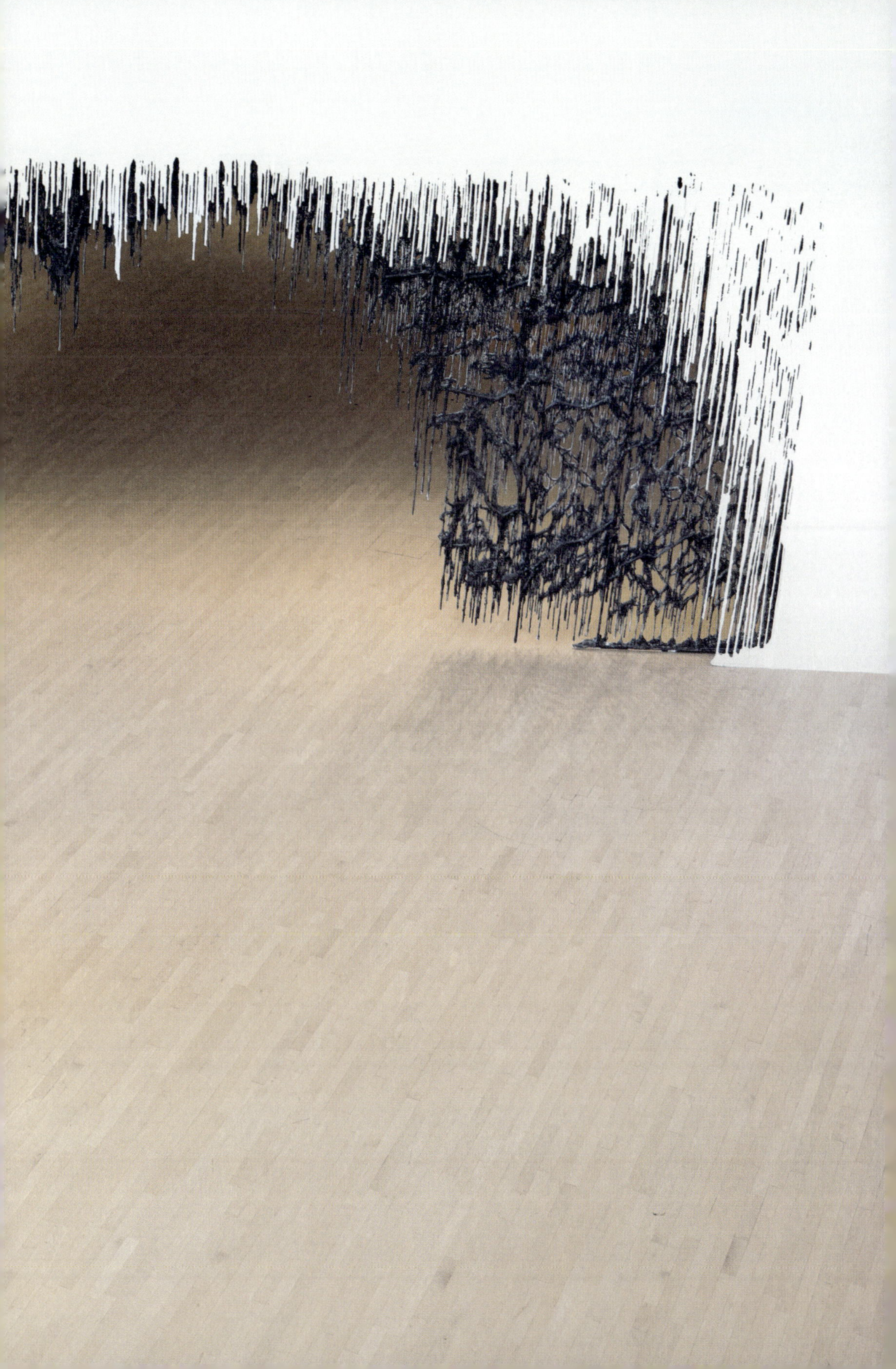

Table of Contents

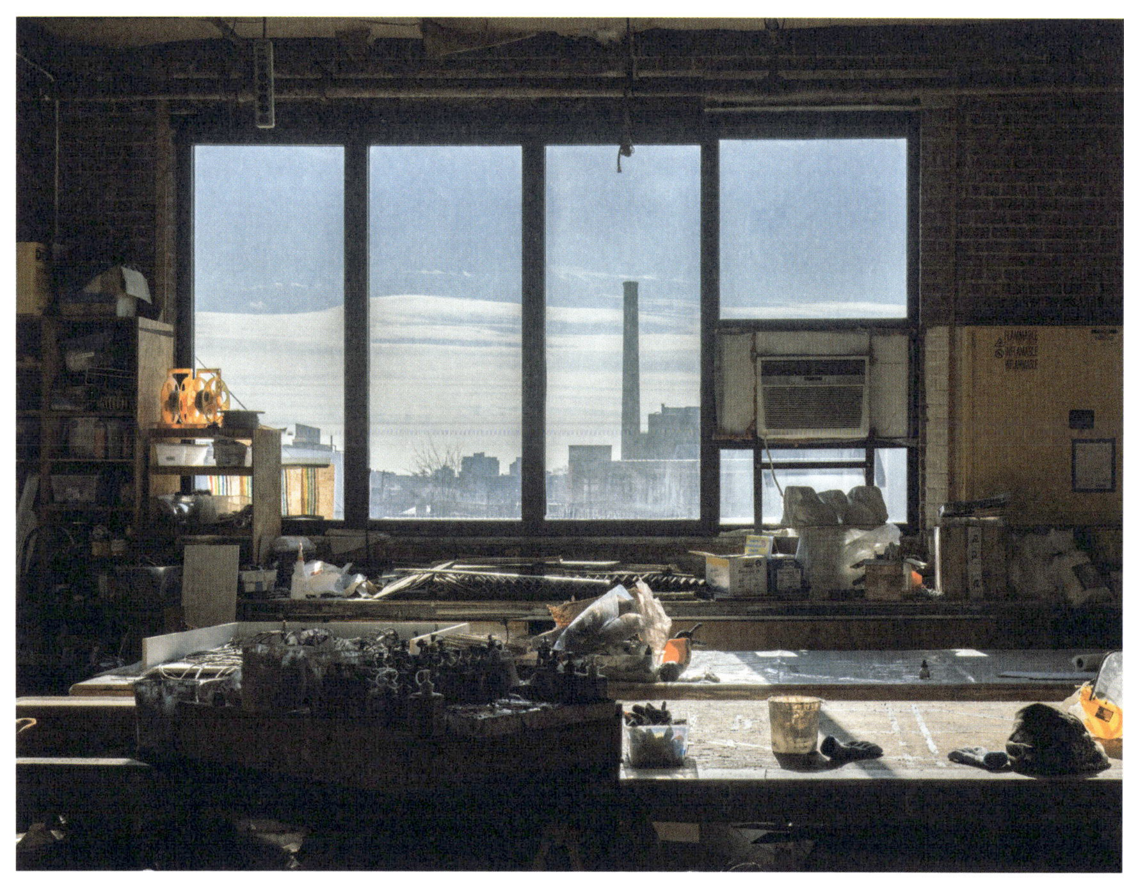

Diana Al-Hadid's studio in Brooklyn, New York.

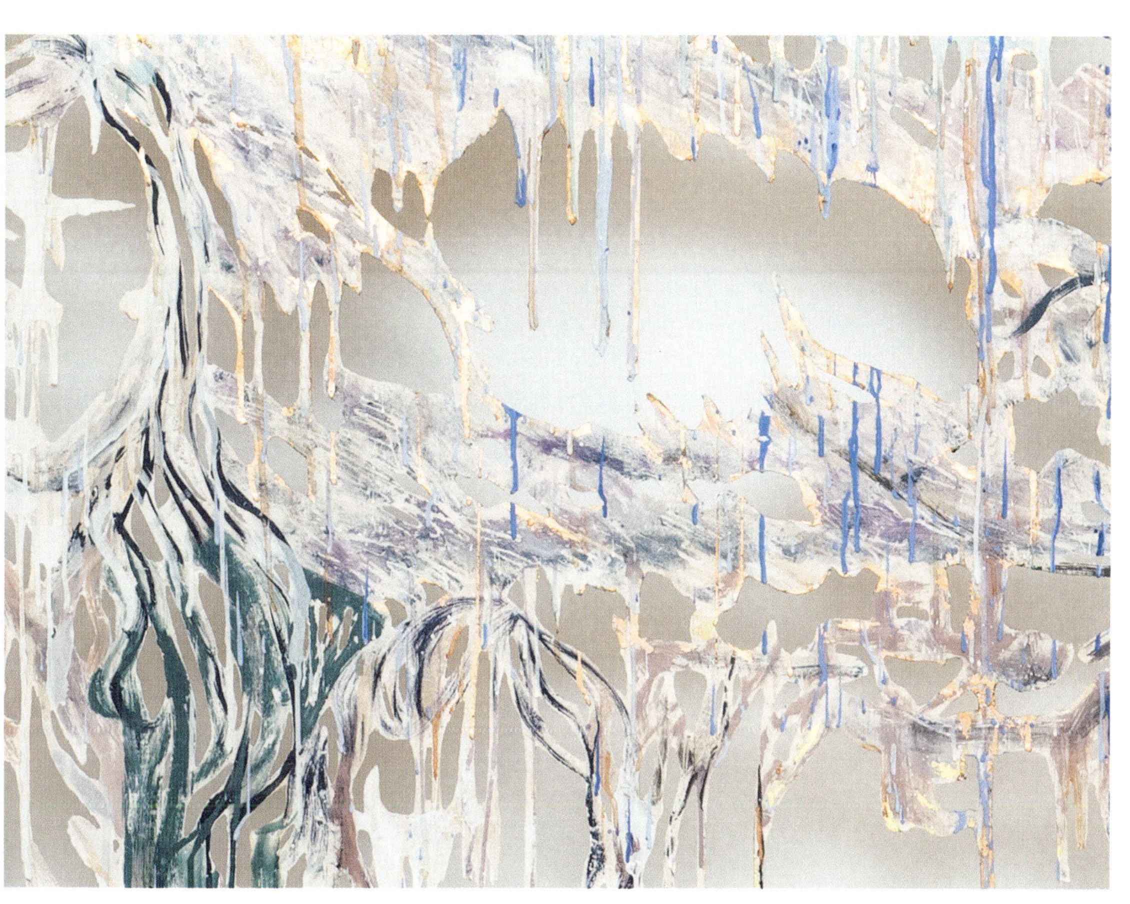

Detail of *August, after The Seventh Month*.

becoming / unbecoming

Rachel Winter, Ph.D.

UNBECOMING: A FRAMEWORK

Diana Al-Hadid's *unbecoming* starts and ends with a self-portrait. The earliest work on view, *Spun of the Limits of my Lonely Waltz* (2006), and the most recent, *August, after The Seventh Month* (2025), take up considerable space, simultaneously asserting and revealing the artist's experiences of becoming and unbecoming at critical life junctures.

Women are told to make themselves scarce, small, quiet, unimportant. To defy this order is to risk being labeled unbecoming, a value judgment reserved for women to signal that which is not—not proper, not appropriate, not acceptable, not becoming.[1] The adjective "becoming" means "suitable, fitting," emphasizing attractiveness and modesty.[2] "Unbecoming" is defined as "not becoming," unflattering, or too much, implying deviations from permissible conduct.[3] The frameworks for unbecoming's meaning are never fixed.

unbecoming is a mid-career survey of work by Syrian American artist Diana Al-Hadid. Across two decades of her practice, Al-Hadid has engaged with questions of gender, womanhood, and femininity while drawing on art history, literature, mythology, and lived experience.[4] The fictional and nonfictional sources informing her work point to moral lessons regarding a woman's character and behavior—ideals that are historically contingent and relentless.

Themes of becoming and unbecoming are intricately embedded in the artist's process. Al-Hadid's work exemplifies the act of becoming: her sculptures take form over time as gestures, lines, marks, and materials accumulate.[5] The artist's signature "drips" of sturdy, rigid materials demonstrate a unique method of fabrication while outlining a decomposition of form, history, and ideology; this visual and conceptual disintegration is integral to its remaking as something unexpected and unbecoming.

Following Al-Hadid's tearing apart of physical, conceptual, and pictorial materials, "unbecoming" evokes a subversive process of transformation: unraveling, falling apart, undoing; it is defiant, revelatory, and filled with potential. "Un" implies a negation, moving backward. Becoming is processual, inching toward a final state. The regression of "un" paired with "becoming" is pivotal, as if one's undoing is integral to growing. Returning to these gendered narratives, Al-Hadid reimagines unbecoming as a mode of agency and an experience of change to be celebrated, one which teaches us about ourselves, where breaking every rule and norm is commended, and falling apart is necessary to coming back together.

UNBECOMING: TAKING UP SPACE

Al-Hadid is keenly attentive to space: how one defines, occupies, and relates to it. Her sculptures quite literally take up space—filling galleries with large-scale installations, prompting viewers to move around or through space to see and activate a work. At moments, the experience and the work can feel overwhelming, too large to comprehend, but scale and detail metaphorically assert the self as worthy of being seen and heard, denying infrastructures of smallness and silence.

pp. 4, 13, 29, 30, 32–33

Spun of the Limits of my Lonely Waltz (2006) (fig. 1) functions as a self-portrait. Made soon after completing her MFA at Virginia Commonwealth University in 2005, and now her earliest extant sculpture, *Spun* began when Al-Hadid waltzed alone in her studio (fig. 2). Residual traces of her footprints formed the work's perimeter, which she then built into a pseudo-Gothic cathedral.[6] Attenuated spires became masses that dwindle like stalactites, and white plaster replaced what would otherwise be colorful glass. *Spun* was then scorched and turned upside down, unsettling the sturdiness of Gothic architecture.

Spun navigates Gothic architecture's magnificent and monstrous duality—a gendered tension. Writer Sheila Heti opens her book *Motherhood* with a similar reflection: "I only knew that I had to create a powerful monster, since I was such a weak one. I had to create a monster apart from me, that knew more than I knew, had a world view…"[7] Inside each woman is a monster: a force that compels her, drives her, pushes her to desire more. Women must restrain this monster, hide her under a polished veneer. Should the monster be unleashed, she is too much.

The monstrous is rarely imagined as potentially an exceptional, earnest form of self, but *Spun* is an exception. By experimenting with and altering Gothic architecture's features, Al-Hadid arrives at

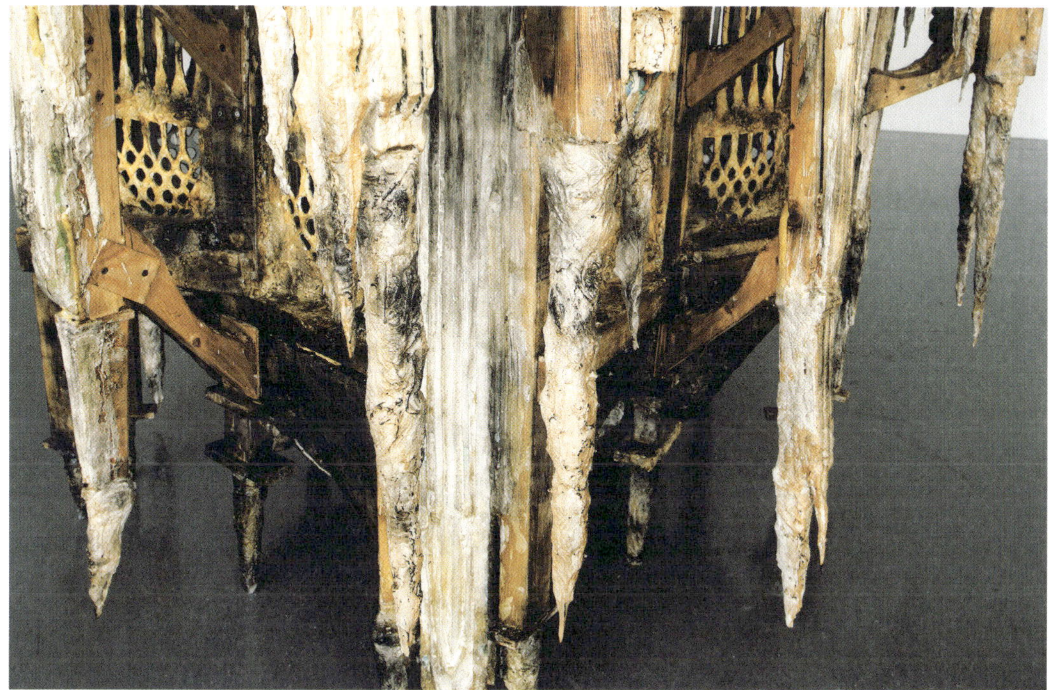

fig. 1   Detail of *Spun of the Limits of my Lonely Waltz*, 2006.

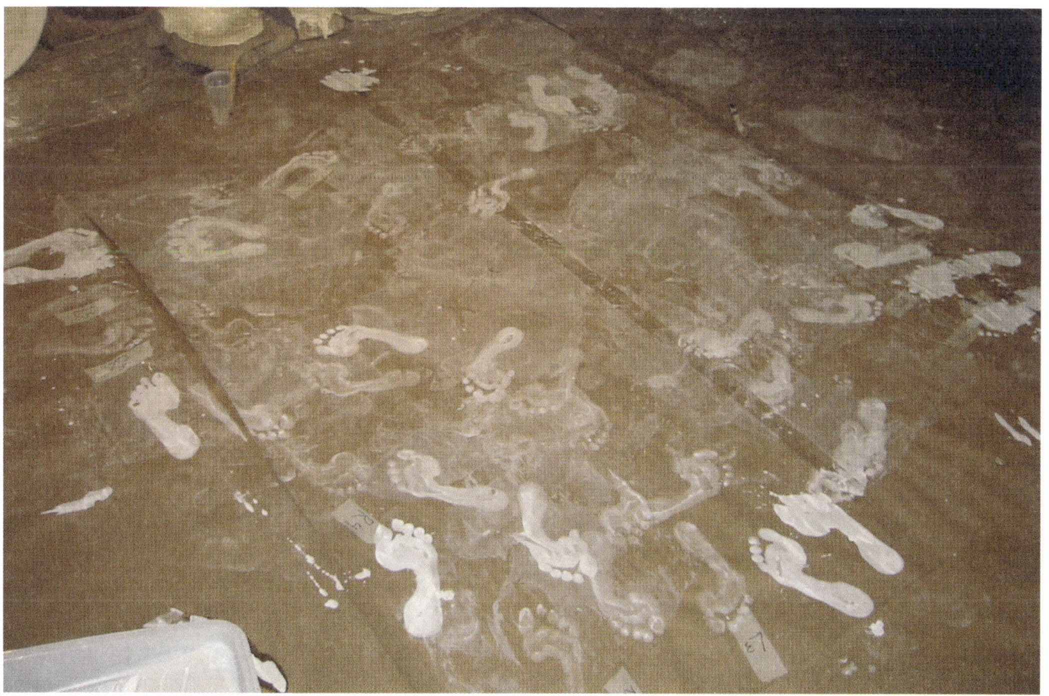

fig. 2   Diana Al-Hadid's studio after dancing the waltz in preparation for *Spun of the Limits of my Lonely Waltz*, 2006.

the monstrous following a journey of unbecoming. The cathedral is a metaphor for the self, a symbol of strength and fortitude found in independence and doing the seemingly unthinkable alone. To visualize this experience, Al-Hadid commands and consumes space, revolting against social norms and art historical conventions of female representation focused on bodies and emotions.

p. 41

Untitled (2014–21) also adopts and adapts art historical references connected to period-specific standards for conduct. A broken bronze mirror floats on a bed of patinaed bronze like a leaf on a body of water discolored by algae, rust, and iron deposits. The mirror draws on Jean-Joseph Perraud's *Lyrical Drama* on the Palais Garnier's façade (fig. 3).[8] Under Napoleon III's modernization campaign, which was imposed on Paris's landscape, the opera house symbolized opulence and cultural refinement. Attending performances there required men and women to follow strict guidelines for suitable appearance and behavior. Al-Hadid shatters this mirror, breaking a symbol of these historical yet incessant systems.

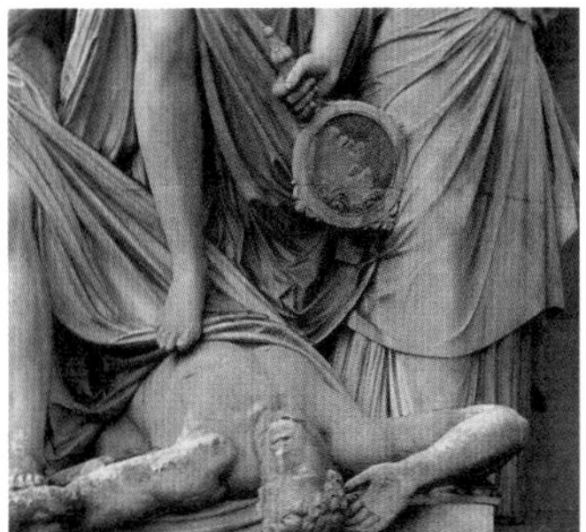

fig. 3   Detail of the mirror in Jean-Joseph Perraud's *Lyrical Drama*, 1865–69, on the façade of the Palais Garnier, Paris.

pp. 4–5, 28–31, 43

Viewers are implicated in these social dynamics in *Smoke Screen* (2015). Inspired by Northern Renaissance paintings in which masses of bodies are carefully organized in pictorial space, Al-Hadid translates these painterly forms into a sculptural entity that acts as a threshold or passageway. Portraits depicting states of repose and congregation are made hollow, outlines of bodies sculpted against a landscape of dripping materials. The scene is frozen in time as the environment decomposes, yet the figures remain static. Viewers activate *Smoke Screen* by moving around and through it while becoming part of the decay they are witnessing.

pp. 42, 45

The perpetual nature of unbecoming is paused in *Mood: 11:14am* (2024). Absent heads and torsos, bodily contours embrace in a state of undress occurring in an abstracted landscape. Al-Hadid's drips are now angled, implying that the bodies are moving in and through a happening, of which only a single instance is pictured. *Mood* subverts tropes from Orientalist paintings of nude women in domestic settings where women are readily available for a man's sexual needs.[9] Such Orientalist scenes feature supposedly exotic and sexually promiscuous women who are of interest for their availability. Al-Hadid upsets this framework by removing details of the female body and adding a male counterpart, thus rendering a more personal scene. Al-Hadid's subject is present yet unavailable, instead embracing intimacy, sexuality, rest, and relaxation while harnessing her agency to find pleasure.

BECOMING: MOTHERHOOD

Central to broader questions of gender and femininity, motherhood is also a recurring theme in Al-Hadid's practice. Women have been formative influences in the artist's life: Her grandmother was a seamstress, and her mother was a florist who still loves working with her hands.[10] The two encouraged Al-Hadid to make and create, something now apparent in the artist's investment in materiality and handmade construction processes.

pp. 36, 39, 91 | pp. 43, 47

Al-Hadid addresses motherhood writ large in *Untitled (Mother Series)* (2023) and *Mother in the Middle* (2023), the latter of which brings the viewer eye to eye with the mother. The maternal figure is monumental, dominating the composition; she is situated on a carpet rendered using the foreshortened perspective of Northern Renaissance paintings. Working across Mylar and handmade paper, Al-Hadid maintains her use of short lines and gestural marks. The mother is present yet ambiguous.

While Al-Hadid's choice of figural scale points to the importance of mothers, abstraction obscures them and pushes them toward invisibility, which reflects social tensions around motherhood. When Sigmund Freud asked, "What do women want?," he thought they wanted to be loved, and the only fitting answer was for women to be mothers.[11] This social expectation persists in which womanhood and motherhood are mutually constituted. Women, however, often face a double bind: Sociological studies describe significant pressure facing working mothers, while women who want a home and family are simultaneously belittled.[12] Should a mother err, she is a monster; finding motherhood unfulfilling is also monstrous.[13] Through abstraction, Al-Hadid points to the paradoxes of motherhood as unrecognized and important, difficult and beautiful, all of which are entangled with becoming—or not becoming—self and mother.

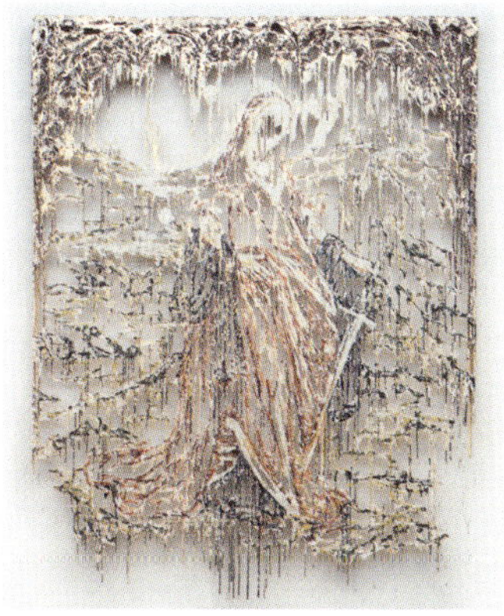

fig. 4   Diana Al-Hadid, *The Seventh Month*, 2015.

pp. 9, 35–37

August, after The Seventh Month (2025) pictures Al-Hadid's own relationship with motherhood, which debuts in *unbecoming*. As the title suggests, *August* follows in the manner of *The Seventh Month* (2015) (fig. 4), a pseudo self-portrait Al-Hadid made when she was seven months pregnant inspired by an image of a woman at the same stage of pregnancy carrying a sword.[14] The expectant mother is evolving, coming apart, as seen in the drips and hollow forms. She is also coming together, growing: her presence commanding, her power indicated by her sword (fig. 5).

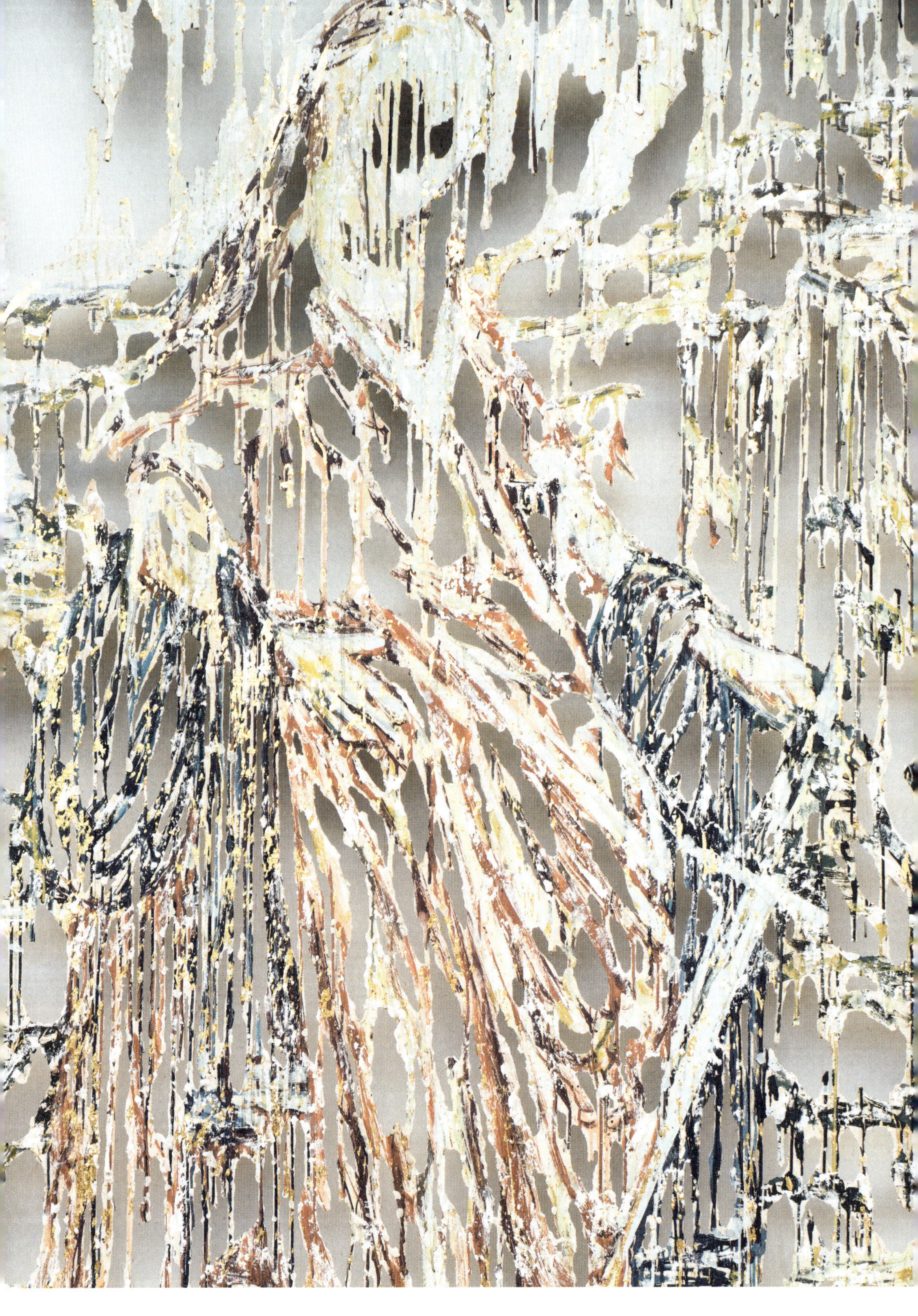

fig. 5   Detail of *The Seventh Month*, 2015.

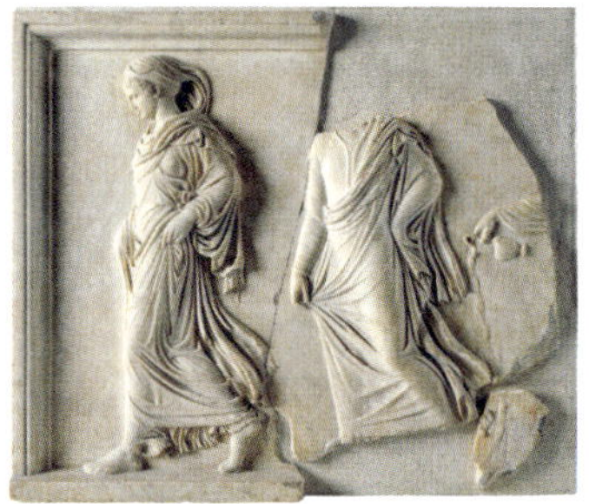

fig. 6   *Gradiva*, originally 5th century CE.

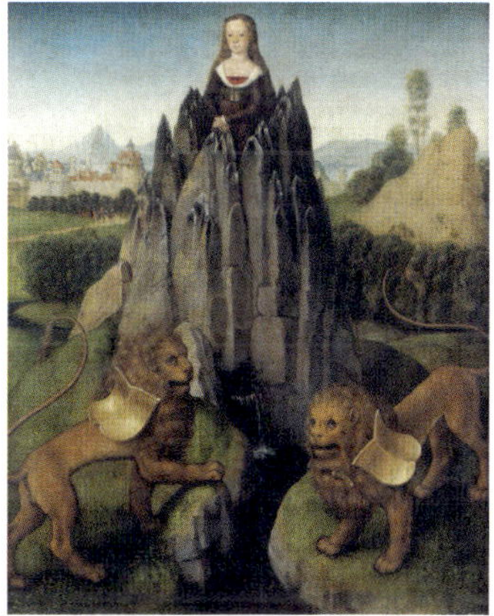

fig. 7   Hans Memling, *Allegory of Chastity*, 1479–80.

pp. 50–51

Ten years later, Al-Hadid reflects in *August*. Her new self-portrait is rendered more naturalistically, conveying strength and certainty; she defines herself contrary to art historical, archetypal, idealized images of mothers. August, her son, stands next to her, holding a toy sword. They are poised within an open landscape that blurs Northern Renaissance painting and a picturesque view of upstate New York. Al-Hadid captures her journey through motherhood in which August is tied to her own transformation. The idea of mother as protector unfolds into an image showing the bond between mother and child—a new rendering of the self that captures a continual becoming and unbecoming.

UNBECOMING: UNAVAILABLE

The story of Gradiva exemplifies how a woman comes into being through male desire. In Wilhelm Jensen's 1903 novella *Gradiva: A Pompeiian Fantasy*, he tells the tale of archaeologist Norbert Hanold who becomes obsessed with a Roman relief depicting a woman walking (fig. 6). The sculpture is named Gradiva, meaning "she who walks."[‡] Hanold's desire for Gradiva consumes him. He travels to Pompeii seeking evidence of her existence. Hanold thinks he finds her and that she's real, but he actually encounters his long-lost childhood love, Zoë Bertgang.[15] Hanold projected his unfulfilled, repressed desires for the unattainable Zoë onto a sculpture and constructed Gradiva.

Al-Hadid has reinterpreted Gradiva throughout her career at varying scales, including intimate drawings like *Untitled* (2013). Al-Hadid outlines Gradiva's silhouette while obscuring her feet, which were important to Hanold's fascination.[16‡‡] As she looks ahead, curved lines replace the folds of her garment and indicate her motion. By rendering Gradiva on Mylar utilizing drips and washes, Al-Hadid depicts her as soft and fluid; she is present yet fleeting and haunting, evoking the way she affected Hanold. This is Gradiva's unbecoming: She is liberated from stone and the archaeologist's ideas of what she should be.

BECOMING: PURITY

Hans Memling's *Allegory of Chastity* (1479–80) has also been a recurring subject in Al-Hadid's oeuvre. Memling's painting features a demure woman with her hands clasped as she looks down (fig. 7). A mountain surrounds her, although it is unclear if the rock imprisons or protects her. Two lions guard her, their importance connoted by the heraldic shields adorning their collars. Memling allegorizes chastity with the amethyst mountain, a symbol of purity vis-à-vis its relation to the color violet.[17] Taken with its landscape, the allegory suggests "virginity or purity" is pivotal to "eternal life."[18] The painting could have been attached to a small female portrait that simultaneously indicated norms and virtues for women.[19] Memling not only pictures the pure and becoming woman, but indicates that her chastity is highly prized and must be protected.

Al-Hadid reinterprets *Allegory of Chastity* to imagine alternative histories and futures for the female protagonist.[20] The artist's first interpretation, *Lionless* (2013), has been described as a playful corrective to Memling's painting.[21] The lions are omitted, as the title states. Memling's earthy landscape dissolves into a subdued, pastel-hued picture where the woman appears to be taking flight, rising above the mountain rather than sinking into it. The colors alter the work's affective nature by reversing the woman's stoicism into a semi-ethereal silhouette. If stone dissolves in *Lionless*, then the mountain fractures into jagged terrain in *Hindsight* (2020). There, the woman floats like an apparition of rage and horror, her elevation indicated through the drips that form her figure while illustrating the mountain's disintegration. The scene is precarious, verging on demonic, as if the woman desires revenge for being imprisoned; in her rage, she is a picture of impropriety. *Deluge in the Allegory* (2020) shifts from the subtle tremors of *Hindsight* to seismic activity. Set within an architectural space, the mountain co-opts the attributes of a volcano as it erupts. The woman's rage is overflowing, but in the deluge, there is a swelling, a freeing, a relief.

Al-Hadid re-envisions both style and iconography, and in turn, narratives around feminine morality, which resonate with broader art historical speculation about authorship and meaning in *Allegory of Chastity*.[22] Each rendition elicits a specific affective state, implicitly questioning the gendered permissibility of emotions. At the artist's hand, the woman redefines her identity, and collectively, the works follow her metamorphosis: seeing and feeling differently, finding rage for change, taking up space, being bold, and eventually, unbecoming.

UNBECOMING: ANGER

Stone and its obdurate qualities shape Al-Hadid's recent work about the mythological figure of Medusa. Caravaggio depicts Medusa aghast and shocked, looking down in horror (fig. 8). Beheaded and disembodied, blood protrudes from her neck, as if her decapitation was

pp. 49, 64, 67

pp. 49, 64–65, 68–69

pp. 49, 65, 71

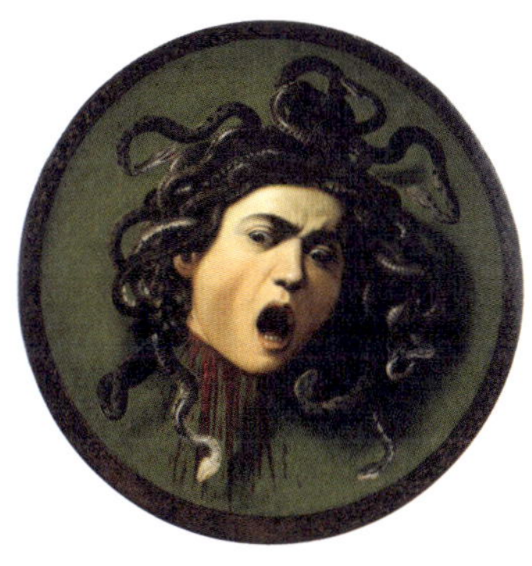

fig. 8   Caravaggio, *Head of Medusa*, 1595–98.

‡
Depictions like these also
displace her maternal nature.

recent. Medusa's hair is composed of intertwined snakes with tongues extended, ready to attack. Caravaggio's interpretation epitomizes many of the common (mis)conceptions about Medusa and her unsuitable features: angry, ugly, prone to destruction.[23]

Although Medusa is one of the most well-known Greek myths, her biography is highly complex. Medusa was one of three Gorgon sisters, but the only mortal one. The god Poseidon raped Medusa, and Athena's punishment for this, whether the sexual encounter was consensual or not, depending on the version of the story, was to turn Medusa into an ugly woman with snakes for hair. Medusa's appearance was said to be so frightening that anyone who met her gaze would turn to stone.[24]‡ Blamed for being a victim, her anger and ugliness is framed as her fault. In other iterations, Medusa is still punished for engaging in consensual sexual activities, and/or her detached head is repurposed for protection. Colloquially, men have also referred to opinionated, vocal women as "Medusa." In the #MeToo movement, survivors have reclaimed Medusa, while feminist reinterpretations have appropriated Medusa as a symbol for anger's capacity to create new beginnings.[25]

Al-Hadid harnesses materiality to represent Medusa's multiplicities: hard and soft, angry and grieving, becoming and unbecoming. The central void of *Blue Medusa* (2023) draws the viewer in, while the scale consumes them. Its circular perimeter recalls apotropaic depictions of Medusa in tondo. Her anguished face is replaced by negative space, and her serpent hair by soft lines like wild curls. Medusa is alive, not frozen in horror, her curves akin to blossoming branches that counter the rigid stone of her lore. In Al-Hadid's depictions of Medusa on paper, her facial features and emotions are more defined. Employing a deeper color palette in *Night Medusa* (2023), lines and drips allude to Medusa's open mouth. The viewer must consider whether she is shocked, angry, or simply speaking, even if unheard.[26] The paper pulp radiates diagonally as if Medusa is growing or exploding. By comparison, *Mad Medusa* (2023) softens the supposedly angry woman toward sorrow, implying the intertwined nature of grief and anger. These are but three examples of portraits in which Al-Hadid tends to Medusa's emotions while freeing her from the stone that confines her (figs. 9–12).

I find *Blue Medusa* pivotal to the framework of *unbecoming*. Medusa exemplifies Al-Hadid's interest in gender and mythology, but I also see her approach to Medusa as modeling different ways of rethinking unbecoming. Women's anger is considered inappropriate or "ugly," no matter the cause, and an indication of a woman's weakness, emotional

pp. 48, 52–53

pp. 48, 54

pp. 48, 55

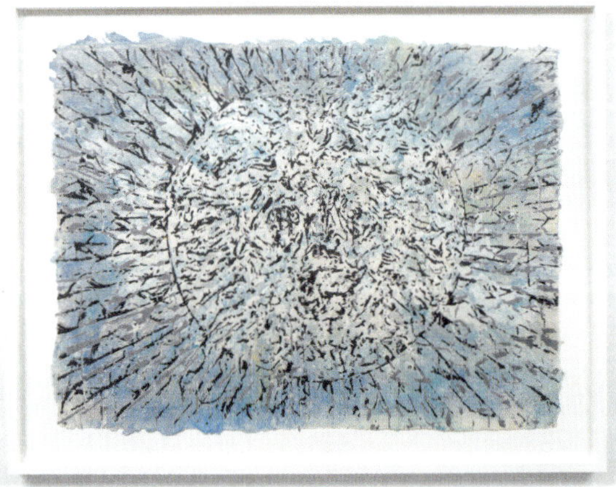

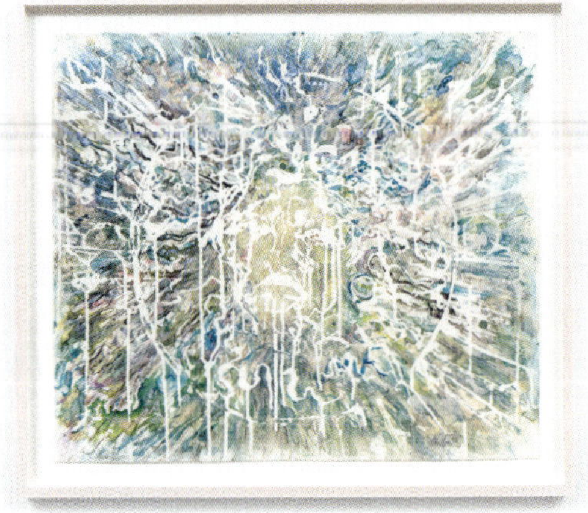

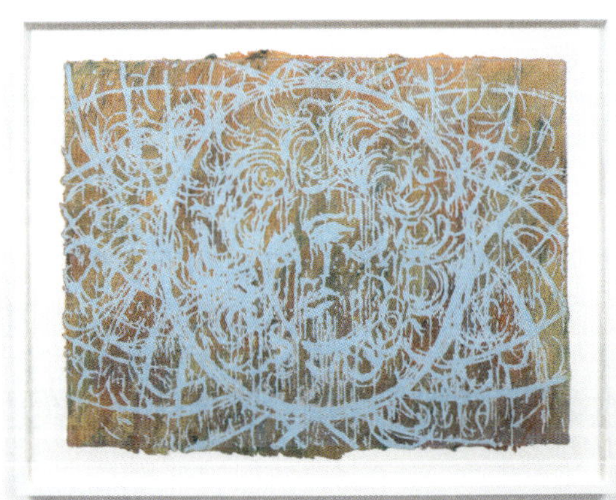

figs. 9–11   In addition to the three images of Medusa discussed in the text, these three works also picture Medusa in relation to different natural elements.

From top: Diana Al-Hadid, *Sky Medusa*, 2023; *Untitled (Medusa)*, 2023; *Medusa Rust*, 2023.

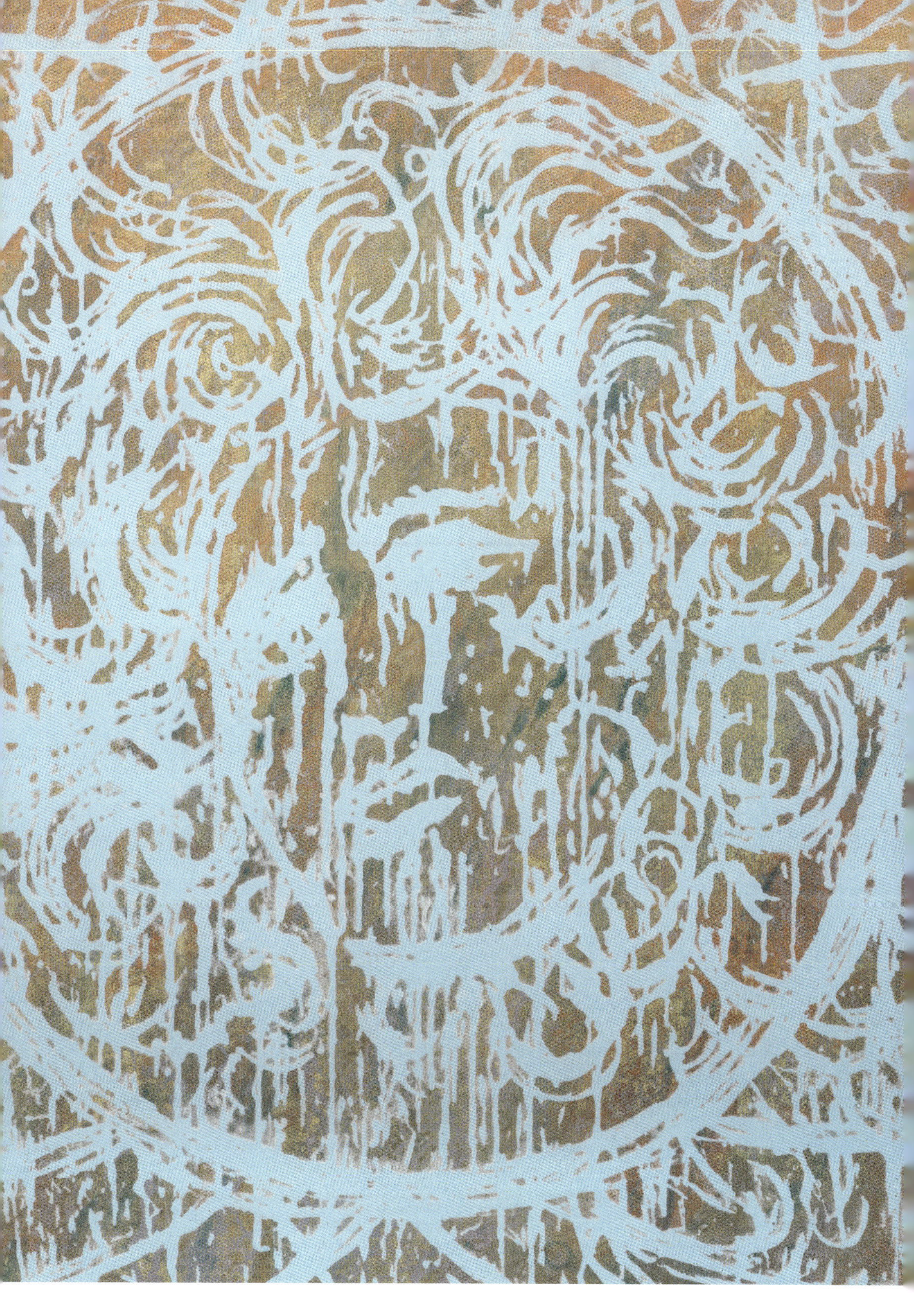

fig. 12   Detail of *Medusa Rust*, 2023.

volatility, and irrationality.[27] Soraya Chemaly explains that when women are told their anger is "undesirable, selfish, powerless, and ugly," it suggests women are the same.[28] ‡ Picturing Medusa as soft, curvaceous, and energetic imagines there is another aspect to women's anger: not as a destructive force, but as a way of grieving that catalyzes change.

BECOMING: SUBSERVIENT

Like *August*, Al-Hadid's new series based on *One Thousand and One Nights* is centered on her self-portrait. In the original *One Thousand and One Nights* or *Arabian Nights*, King Shahryar is enraged after finding his wife was unfaithful. As revenge against all womankind, he takes a new wife every night and ends her life the next morning before she can wrong him. Scheherazade, the protagonist, valiantly volunteers to be the king's next wife. She goes to his residence with her sister Dunyazad, who watches nearby as Scheherazade tells the king stories to keep him occupied, which saves her life.[29] Elsewhere in this volume, Al-Hadid elaborates on the power of Scheherazade's art and creativity.

Situated within an abstract, imaginary landscape, Al-Hadid presents three scenes of storytelling focused on the protagonist, and the works' titles indicate three of the story's components. First, in *There was and* pp. 49, 57, 61, 82–83 *there was not... a foolish king* (2025), Al-Hadid references King Shahryar by name, a man who is pivotal to the tales but who is not visually represented in Al-Hadid's interpretation. Second, the title *There was* pp. 24, 48–49, 56, 58–59 *and there was not... two sisters who lived in the trees* (2025) refers to the story's leading ladies: Scheherazade and Dunyazad. Al-Hadid's younger brother Sam takes Dunyazad's place, reclining on his mother's couch nearing sleep. Sam's presence is a double form of displacement that echoes feminist re-readings of the tales: he occupies the pictorial space formerly allocated to the king; and he alludes to the king's brother, who in the original tales, also avenged his wife for infidelity.[30] Third, pp. 49, 56–57, 60, 62–63 *There was and there was not... a clever woman in disguise* (2025), a title that describes the story's protagonist. This woman is Al-Hadid, who pictures herself as Scheherazade while assuming the position of storyteller and listener, her ingenuity enabling her to distract the king from his tirade.

Al-Hadid's study of Scheherazade also harkens back to her early career. Soon after finishing graduate school, Al-Hadid made *Finally, the Emancipation of Scheherazade* (2006) (fig. 13), which juxtaposes tropes of protection and critiques of Orientalist representation.[31] A small

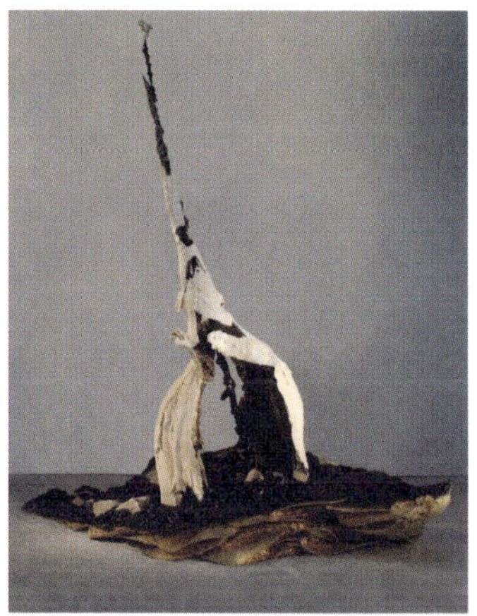

fig. 13   Diana Al-Hadid, *Finally, the Emancipation of Scheherazade*, 2006. No longer extant.

golden lamp, like the genie's in the story of Aladdin, pours a black, oil-like substance that dissolves into other materials. In the middle, a small evil eye serves as a protective emblem. Underneath a pseudo-oil spill are scalloped layers of gold inscribed with Arabic calligraphy. These features are typical of Orientalist ideas about the Arab world connected to pop culture stereotypes and misrepresentations of the region. As the title suggests, we see Scheherazade's "emancipation," upright and ready to flee, but it is unclear how she is freed.

In the new series, Scheherazade is reimagined as an archetype of female agency, strength, and perseverance who frees herself. Underpinning *One Thousand and One Nights* is a troubling lesson about how women suffer under the oppressive constraints of fidelity and purity imposed by men.[32] Enter the beautiful and charismatic Scheherazade, preemptively condemned for her assumed future infidelity. Yet she can also be considered an unreliable narrator; her stories are a decoy, and so is she, as indicated in Al-Hadid's contradictory series title, *There was and there was not...*[33] ‡ She subverts and endures a perilous system in a cunning act of deception that eventually saves her and womankind. Scheherazade shows the power of unbecoming as a tool of survival and change.

UNBECOMING: AN ASPIRATION

In the gendered stories entangled with Al-Hadid's work, much like the sculptures themselves, we find tenacity and resilience. Materials accumulate to their breaking point, forms consume rooms and demand our bodily engagement while pushing the capacity of a space to its limits; their unbecoming reveals a site of potentiality and transformation, demanding us to think and see differently through the unexpected. While at first glance, the work may seem too much to comprehend or seem to resist quick glances and passive ways of looking, Al-Hadid's work is suitable, fitting—becoming.

I can also think about moments in which I have been deemed too much, unbecoming. But I have learned, in part through the making of this exhibition, to embrace the unbecoming, to find in it a powerful tool for envisioning an alternative future and the most magnificent form of self. ◆

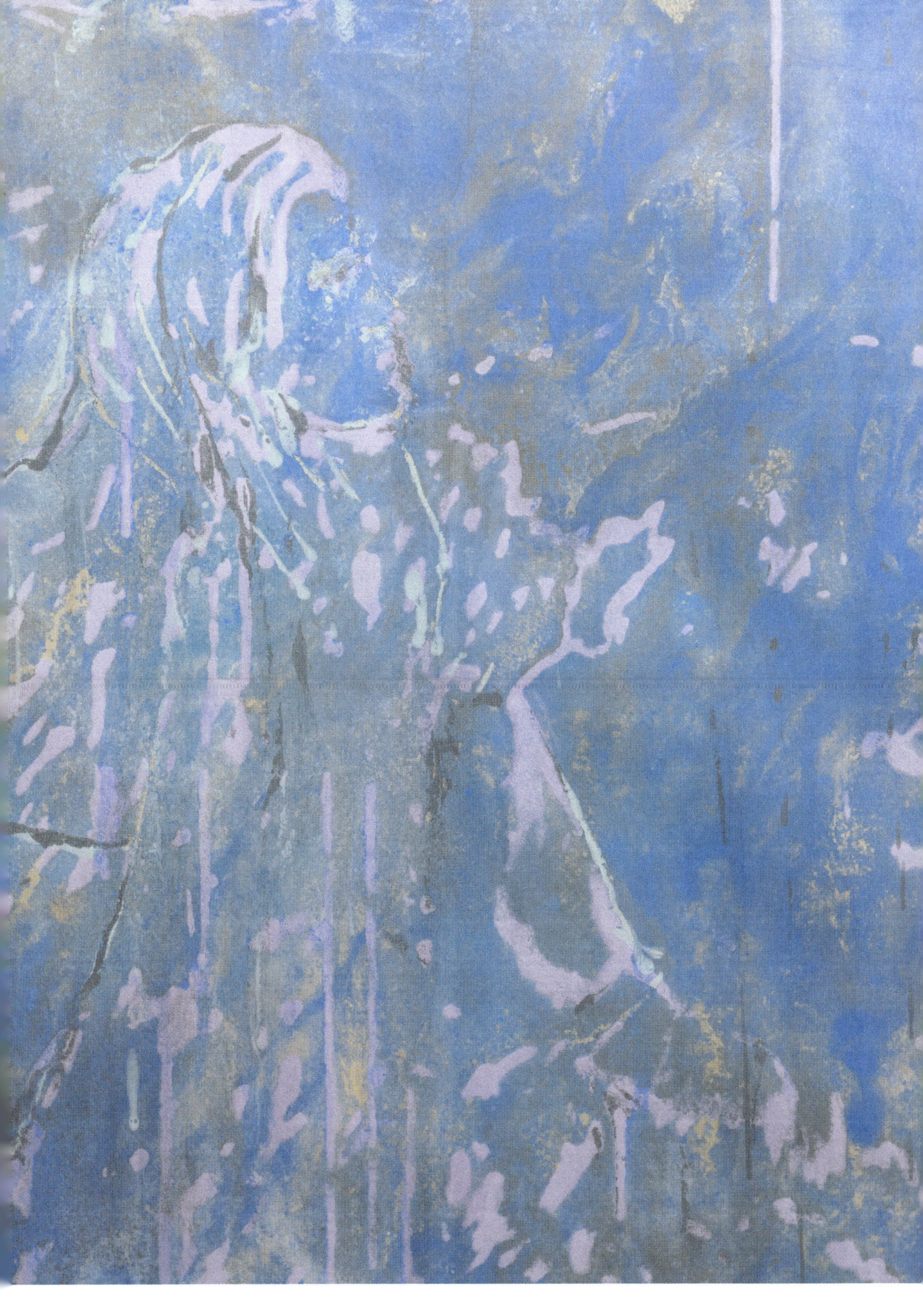

Detail of *There was and there was not... two sisters who lived in the trees*, 2025.

1. For example: Susan Fraiman, *Unbecoming Women: British Women Writers and the Novel of Development* (Columbia University Press, 1993); Therese Oneill, *Unbecoming a Lady: The Forgotten Sluts and Shrews Who Shaped America* (Simon & Schuster, 2024); Cristina Santos, *Unbecoming Female Monsters: Witches, Vampires, and Virgins* (Lexington Books, 2016).

2. "Becoming," Merriam Webster, last updated May 23, 2025, https://www.merriam-webster.com/dictionary/becoming. This usage dates to the sixteenth century.

3. "Unbecoming," Merriam Webster, last updated April 22, 2025, https://www.merriam-webster.com/dictionary/unbecoming. Similar value judgments include: audacious, too much, hysterical, or monstrous. See: Jennifer Cooke, *Contemporary Feminist Life-Writing: The New Audacity* (Cambridge University Press, 2020), 17; Rachel Vorona Cote, *Too Much: How Victorian Constraints Still Bind Women Today* (Grand Central Publishing, 2020), 292; Jess Zimmerman, *Women and Other Monsters: Building a New Mythology* (Beacon Press, 2021).

4. Gender has also been the focus of exhibitions like *Diana Al-Hadid: Delirious Matter* at Madison Square Park (May 14–September 3, 2018), *Archive of Longings* at the Henry Art Gallery, University of Washington (October 2, 2021–February 6, 2022), and *Women, Bronze, and Dangerous Things* at Kasmin Gallery (November 2–December 22, 2023).

5. Mary Kelly, "Locating the First Sculptural Mark: An Artist Interview with Diana Al-Hadid," in *Under the Skin: Feminist Art and Art Histories from the Middle East and North Africa Today*, ed. Ceren Özpınar and Mary Kelly (Oxford University Press, 2020), 177–78; "Diana Al-Hadid," in *Being an Artist: Artist Interviews with Art21* (Art21, 2018), 195–98.

6. Kelly, "Locating the First Sculptural Mark," 181; Sharon Hecker, "Walking Through Walls: Medardo Rosso and Diana Al-Hadid," in *Diana Al-Hadid: Regarding Medardo Rosso* (Marianne Boesky Gallery, 2016), 30; Jed Morse, *Sightings: Diana Al-Hadid* (Nasher Sculpture Center, 2011), 2; Alistair Rider, "The Skin is a Screen," in *Phantom Limb*, ed. Maya Allison (Skira, 2016), 44–45.

7. Sheila Heti, *Motherhood* (Alfred A. Knopf, 2018), 1–2.

8. Hecker, "Walking Through Walls," 24. On the opera house's sculptural program, see: Christopher Curtis Mead, *Charles Garnier's Paris Opéra: Architectural Empathy and the Renaissance of French Classicism* (MIT Press, 1991).

9. See: Linda Nochlin, "The Imaginary Orient," in *The Politics of Vision* (Harper & Row, 1989), 33–57.

10. "Diana Al-Hadid," in *Art Studio America*, ed. Hossein Amirsadeghi, et. al. (Thames & Hudson, 2013), 70.

11. Margarita Cereijido, "What Do Women Want Today?," in *Psychoanalytic Explorations of What Women Want Today: Femininity, Desire and Agency*, ed. Margarita Cereijido, Paula L. Ellman, and Nancy R. Goodman (Routledge, 2022), 3–9.

12. Francesco Nicola Maria Petricone, *Women Today: Comparative Sociological-Juridical Research on Gender Inequality* (Mimesis International, 2022), 42.

13. Santos, *Unbecoming Female Monsters*, xxi; Ruby Warrington, *Women Without Kids: The Revolutionary Rise of an Unsung Sisterhood* (Sounds True, 2024), 2–3.

14. Monica Ramirez-Montagut, "Diana Al-Hadid: An Interview," in *Diana Al-Hadid* (Newcomb Museum of Art, 2016), 9–13.

15. Mary Bergstein, *Mirrors of Memory: Freud, Photography, and the History of Art* (Cornell University Press, 2010), 116–17. Gradiva is sometimes also translated as "she who walks through walls."

16. The feet had an erotic connotation in late nineteenth-century Vienna. See: Mary Bergstein, *Visual Culture in Freud's Vienna: Science, Eros, and the Psychoanalytic Imagination* (Bloomsbury, 2024), 122.

17. Barbara Lane, *Hans Memling: Master Painter in Fifteenth-Century Bruges* (Harvey Miller, 2009), 330.

18. Dirk De Vos, *Hans Memling: The Complete Works* (Ludion Press, 1994), 164.

19. Alison Manges Nogueira, "Uncovering Renaissance Portraits," in *Hidden Faces: Covered Portraits of the Renaissance* (The Metropolitan Museum of Art, 2024), 33. While Nogueira argues this was likely the reverse, scholars contest this. See: Till-Holger Borchert, "Looking at Memling Through the Eyes of our Time," in *Memling Now: Hans Memling in Contemporary Art* (Musea Brugge, 2020), 19.

20. For a broader study of Al-Hadid's interpretations of *Allegory of Chastity*, see: Aruna D'Souza, "In Media Res," in *Memling Now: Hans Memling in Contemporary Art* (Musea Brugge, 2020), 47–58.

21. "Diana Al-Hadid: Sublimations," Frist Art Museum, accessed March 2025, https://fristartmuseum.org/exhibition/diana-al-hadid-sublimations/.

22. De Vos, *Hans Memling*, 164; Lane, *Hans Memling*, 330; Borchert, "Looking at Memling," 19.

23. Depictions like these also displace her maternal nature. See: Adriana Cavarero, *Horrorism: Naming Contemporary Violence* (Columbia University Press, 2008), 14–18.

24. Marjorie B. Garber and Nancy J. Vickers, eds., *The Medusa Reader* (Routledge, 2003), 2.

25. Jennifer Hedgecock, *Cultural Reflections of Medusa: The Shadow in the Glass* (Routledge, 2020), 2–8.

26. Gayatri Chakravorty Spivak, "Can the Subaltern Speak?," in *Marxism and the Interpretation of Culture*, ed. Cary Nelson and Lawrence Grossberg (Macmillan, 1988), 271–313.

27. Cecile R. Bassen, "The Persistent Impact of Stereotypes about Women," in *Psychoanalytic Explorations of What Women Want Today: Femininity, Desire and Agency*, ed. Margarita Cereijido, Paula L. Ellman, and Nancy R. Goodman (Routledge, 2022), 118; Nancy Colier, *The Emotionally Exhausted Woman: Why You're Feeling Depleted and How to Get What you Need* (New Harbinger Publications, 2022), 104–8.

28. Soraya Chemaly, *Rage Becomes Her: The Power of Women's Anger* (Atria Books, 2018), 25. Al-Hadid has also reflected on anger, noting in an interview "A lot of the time women are tasked with keeping it all together for everyone else, being calm and in control; yet, when we're legitimately angry, we're the volcano—there's something there that's both empowering and infuriating. We can't drop the ball and we can't miss a beat; I have this feeling both as a woman and as an immigrant." See: Kelly, "Locating the First Sculptural Mark," 187.

29. For a more expansive history, see Dwight F. Reynolds, "*A Thousand and One Nights*: A History of the Text and Its Reception," in *Arabic Literature in the Post-Classical Period*, ed. Roger Allen and D. S. Richards (Cambridge University Press, 2006), 270–92; and Paulo Lemos Horta, *Marvellous Thieves: Secret Authors of the Arabian Nights* (Harvard University Press, 2017).

30. Daniel E. Beaumont, *Slave of Desire: Sex, Love, and Death in The 1001 Nights* (Fairleigh Dickinson University Press, 2002); Seda Demiralp, "1001 Nights with Animus," *Arab Studies Quarterly* 43, no. 3 (Summer 2021): 213–29.

31. Hecker, "Walking Through Walls," 29–30; Sara Raza, "Diana Al-Hadid: Suspended Informal Architectures in Time and Space," in *Phantom Limb*, ed. Maya Allison (Skira, 2016), 56–57; Robin Reisenfeld, "The Labyrinth in the Tower: A Conversation with Diana Al-Hadid," *Sculpture* 28, no. 2 (March 2009): 28–29.

32. On the centrality of purity and fidelity to *One Thousand and One Nights*, see: Ismat Latif Mehdi, "Modern Sheharzads: Women as Storytellers," and Ashfaq Ahmad, "Woman in Islamic Society: A Study of *The Arabian Nights*," in *Essays on the Arabian Nights*, ed. Rizwanur Rahman and Syed Akhtar Husain (Primus Books, 2015).

33. The title *There was and there was not...* is a literal translation of *Kān ya ma kān*, which colloquially also means "once upon a time."

Exhibition and Plates

June 7–December 14, 2025
MSU Broad Art Museum

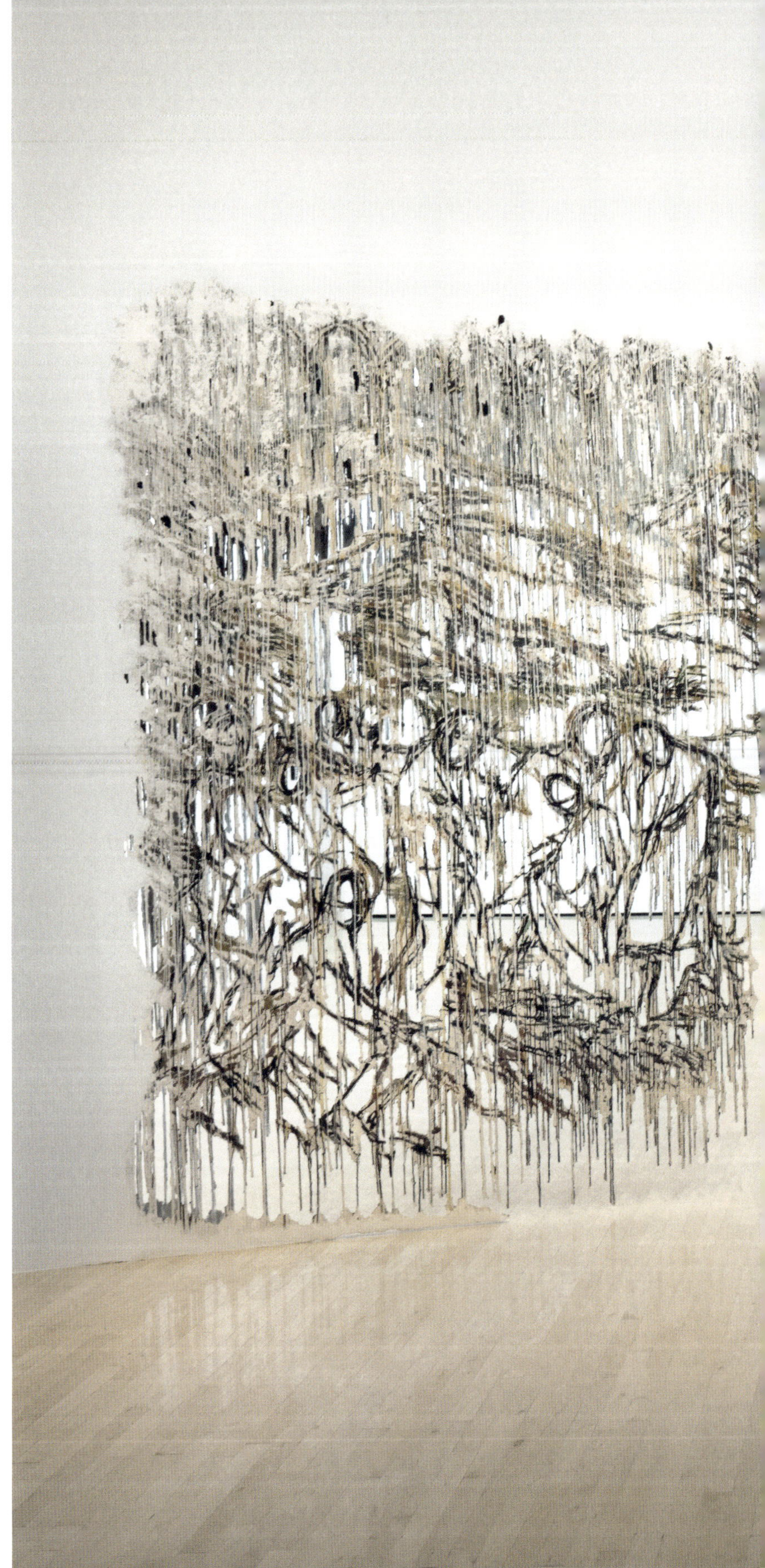

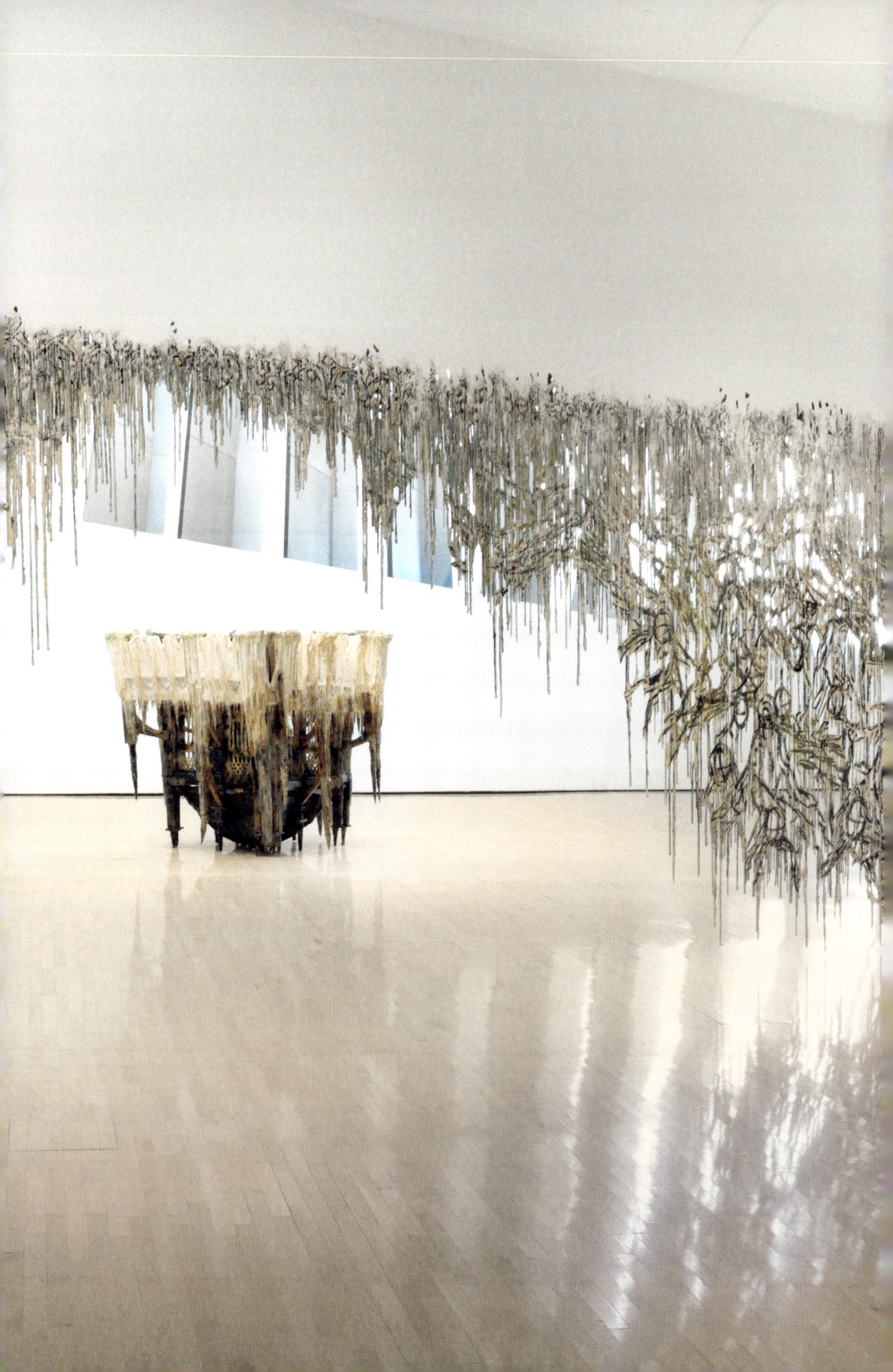

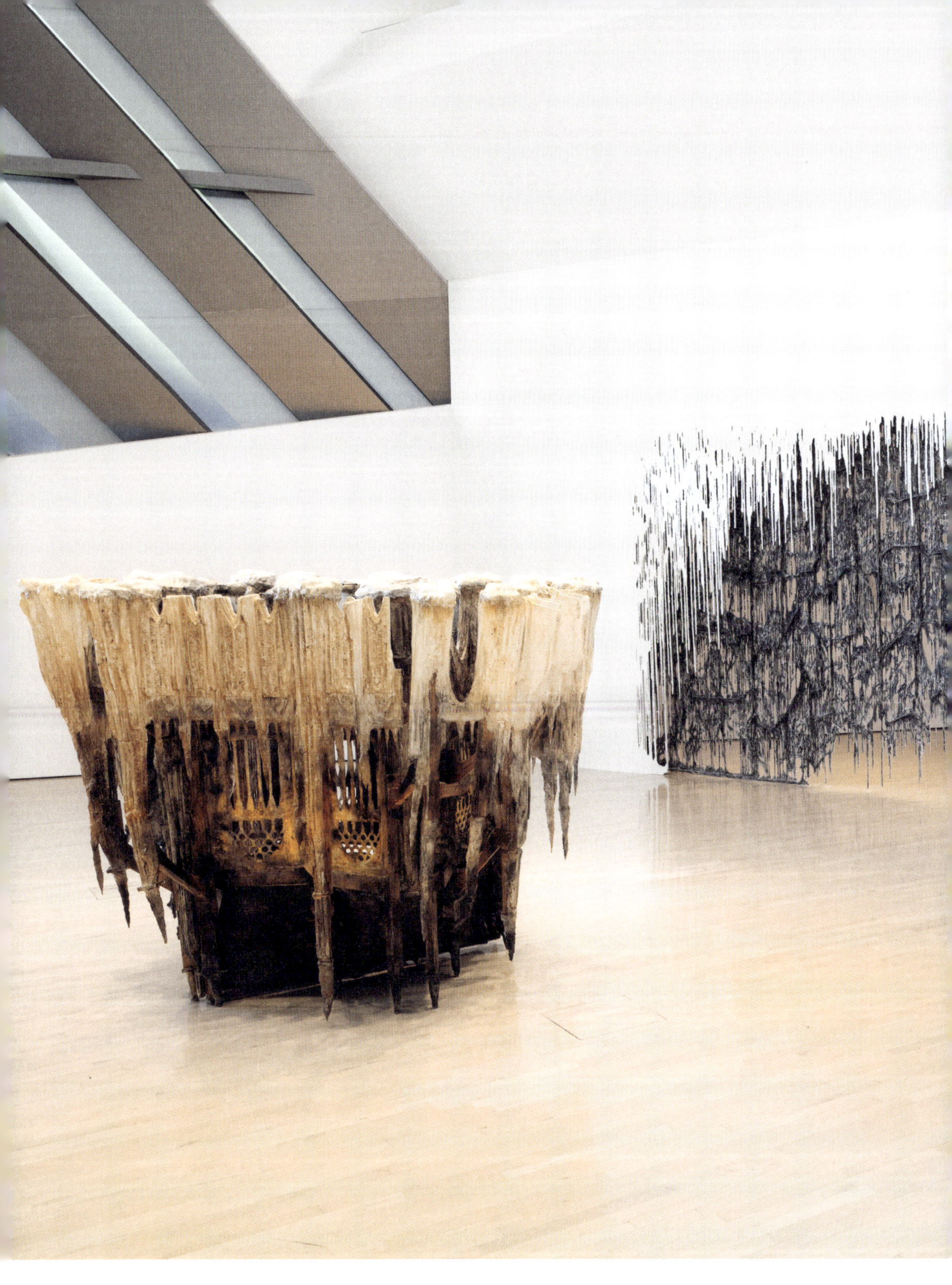

Spun of the Limits of my Lonely Waltz, 2006
wood, polystyrene, plaster, fiberglass, and pigment

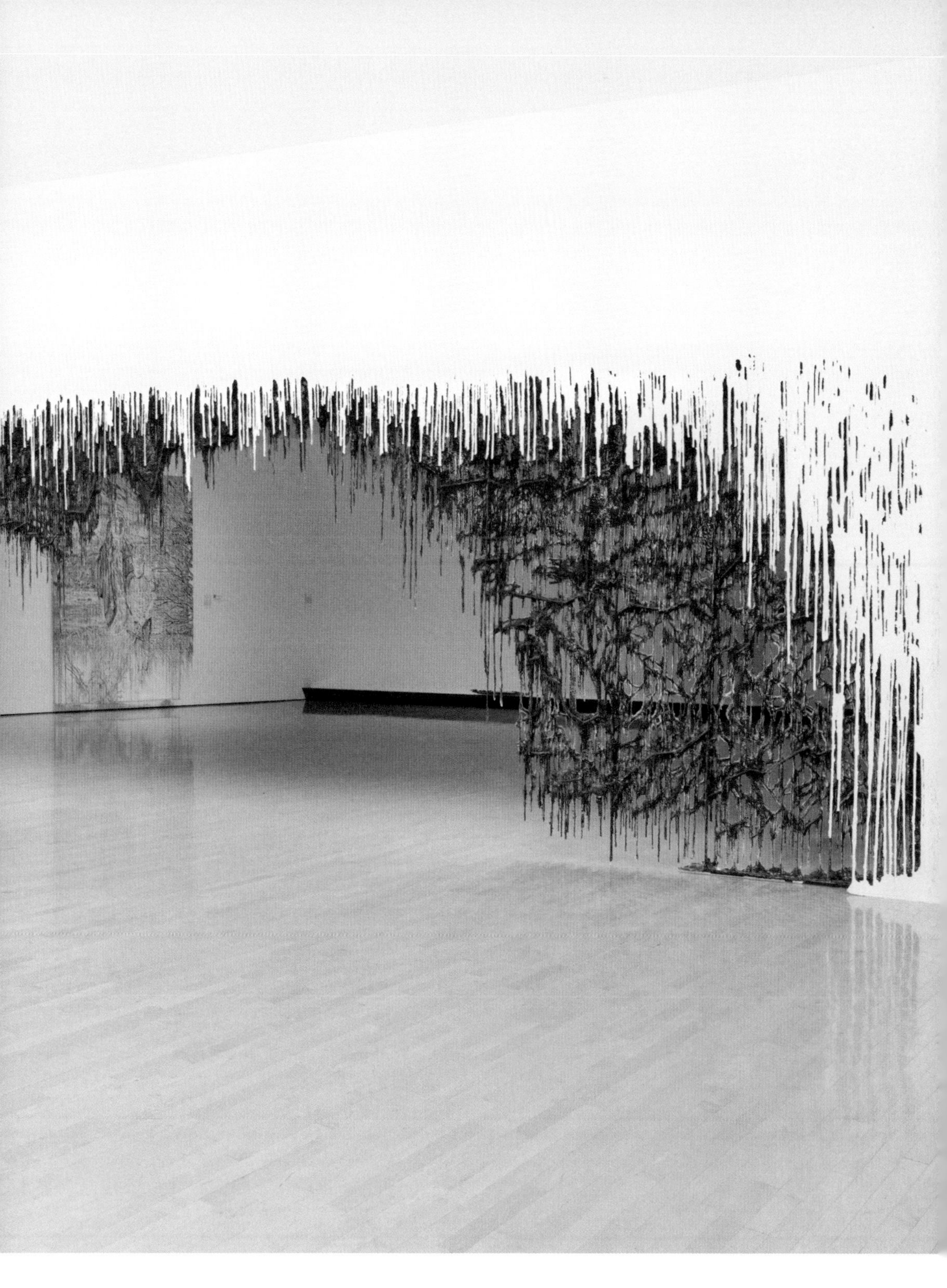

Smoke Screen, 2015
polymer gypsum, fiberglass, steel, gold leaf, plaster, and pigment

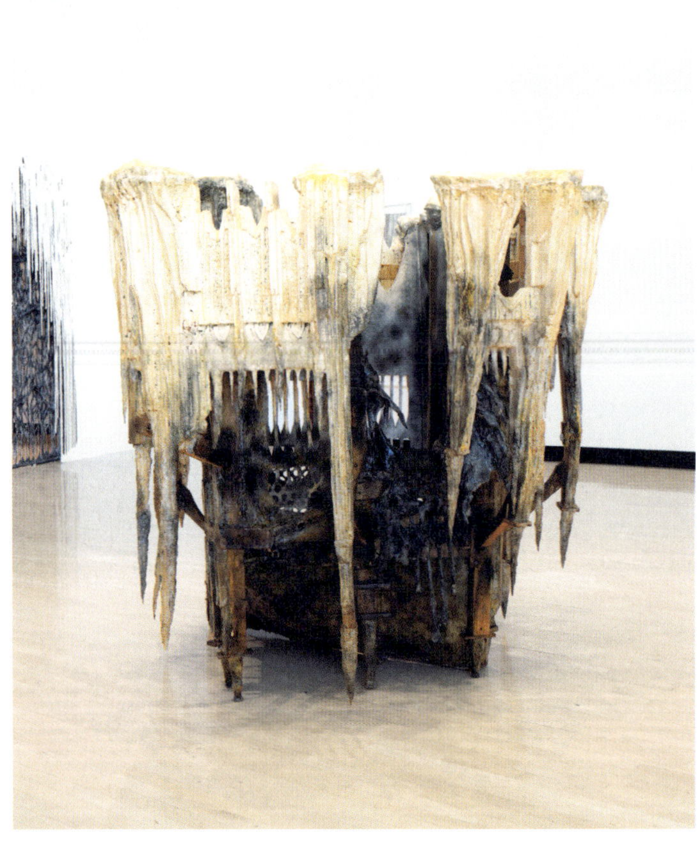

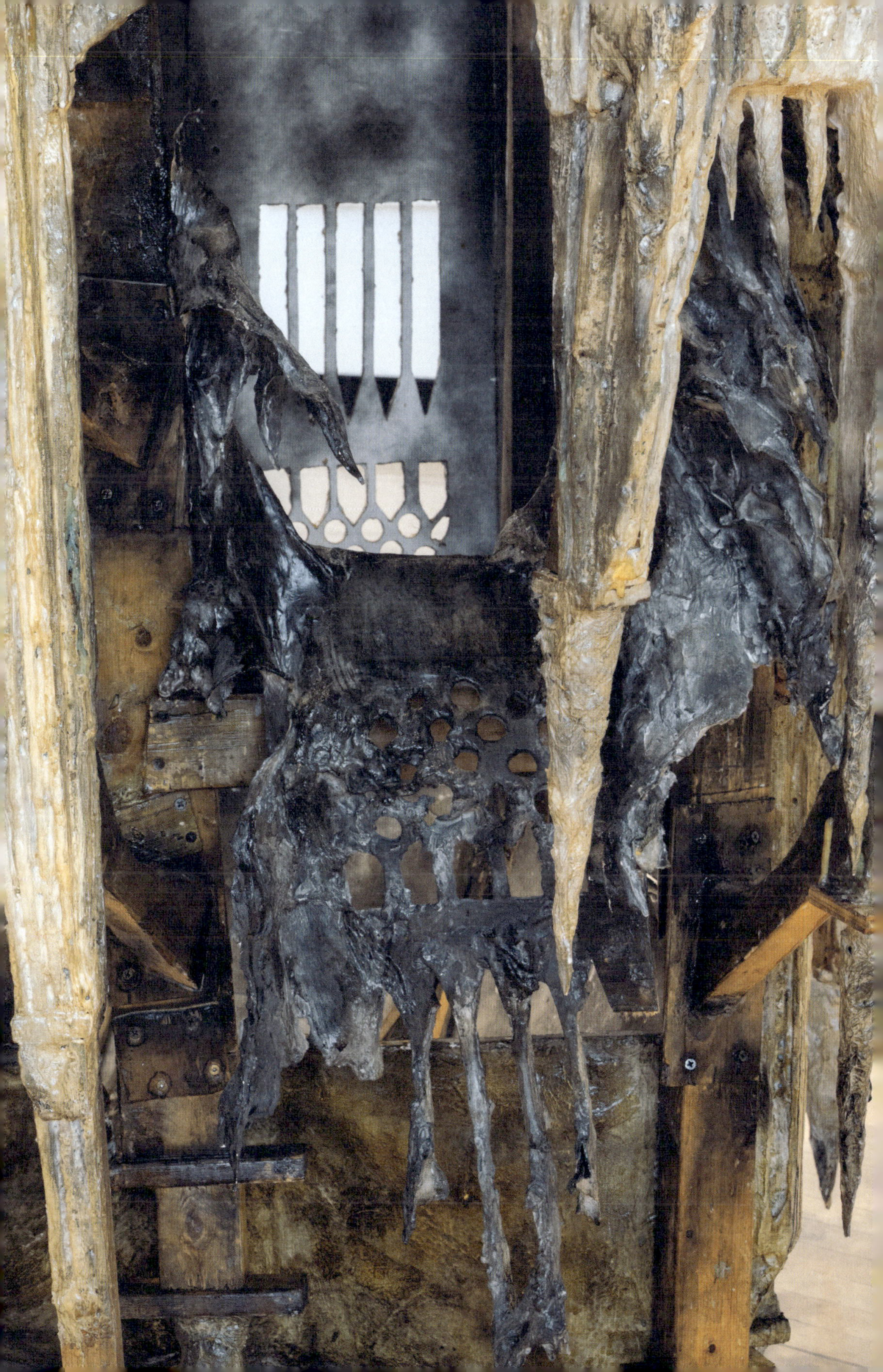

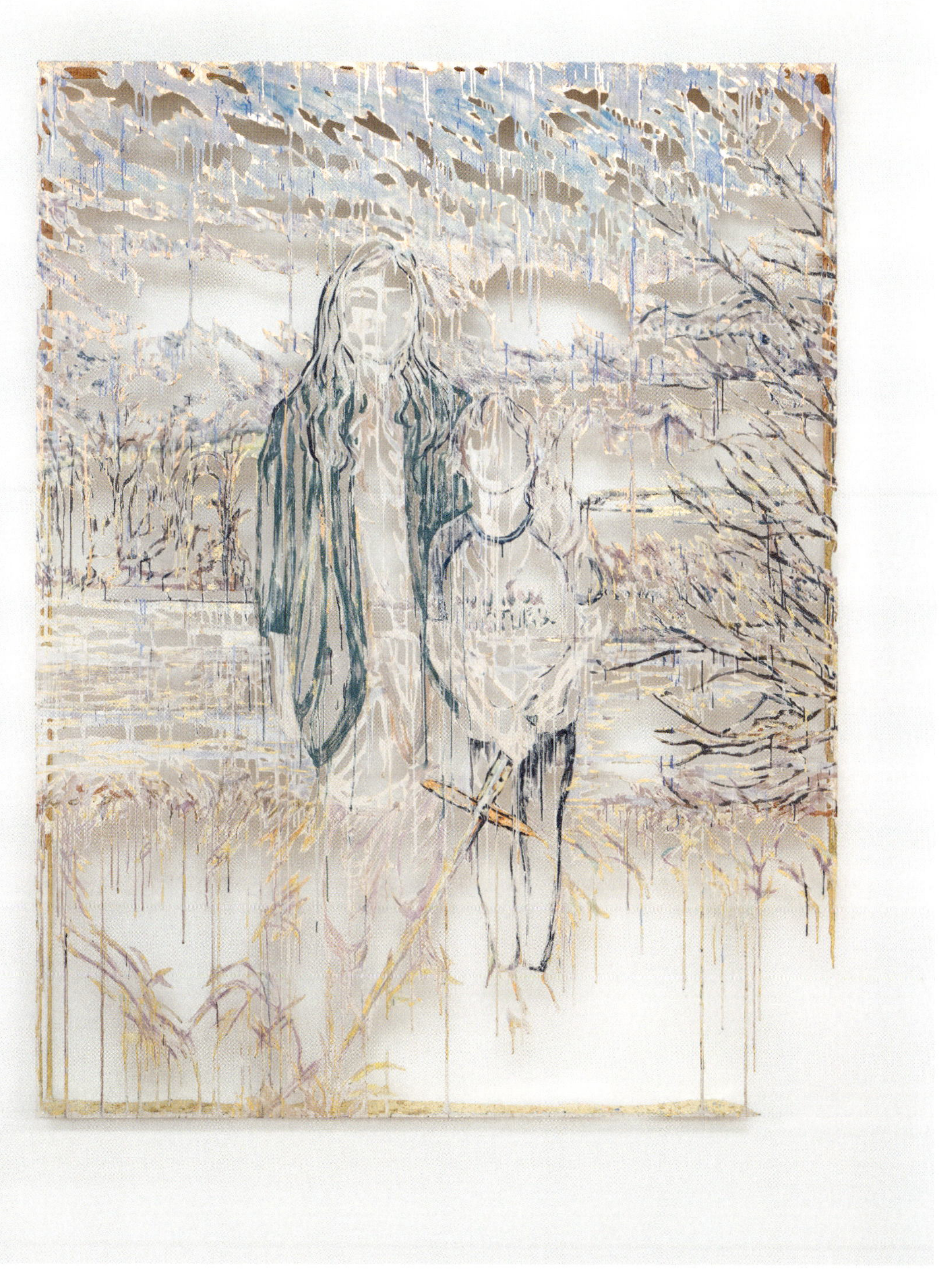

August, after The Seventh Month, 2025
polymer gypsum, fiberglass, steel, plaster, metal leaf, and pigment

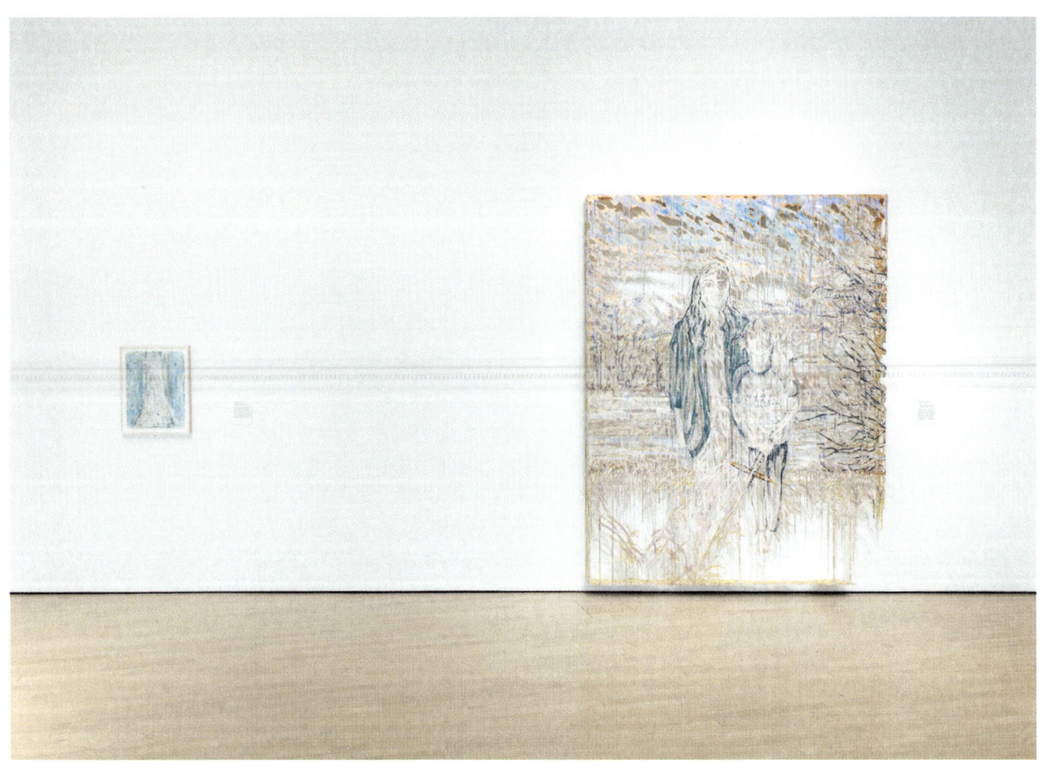

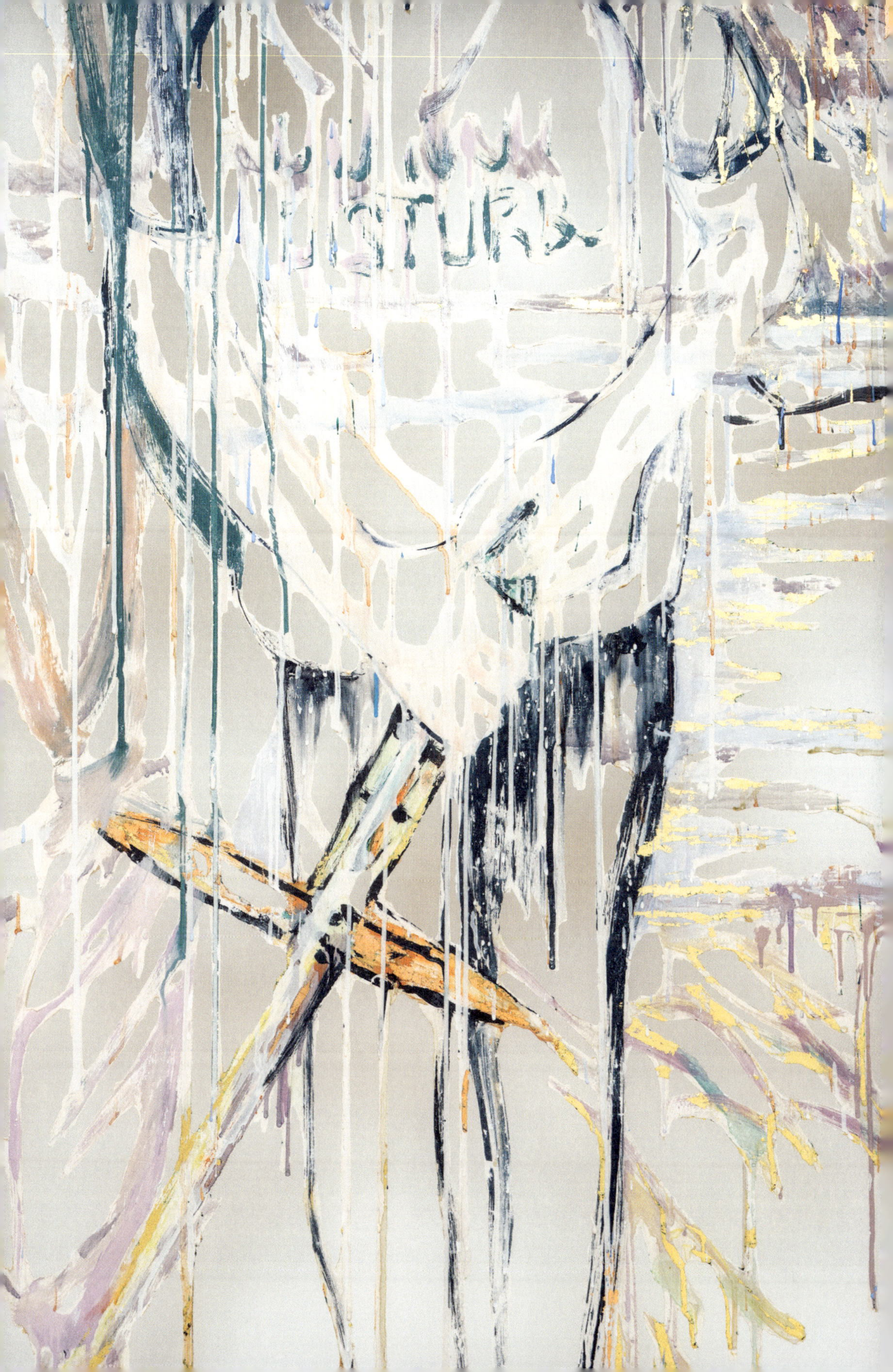

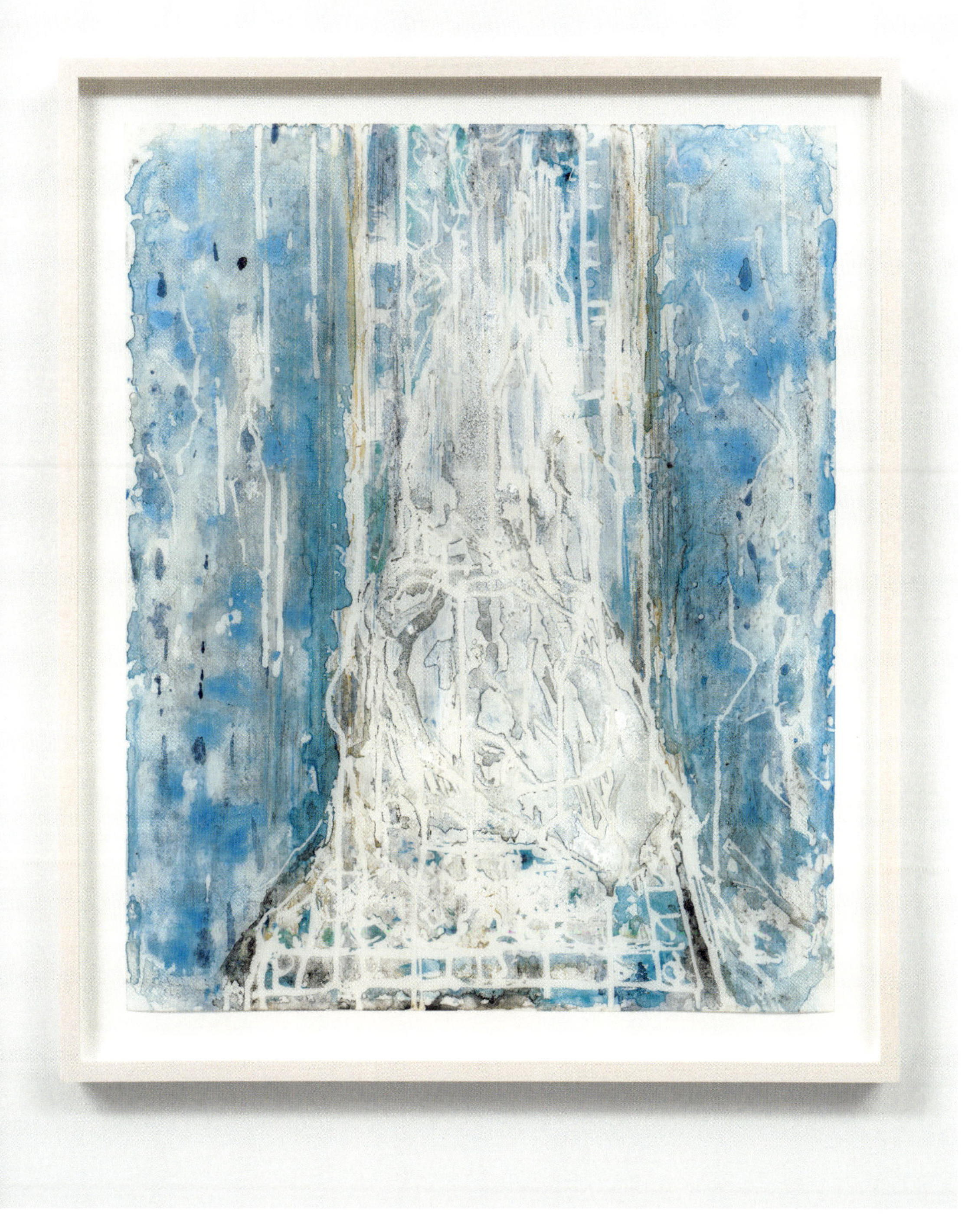

Untitled (Mother Series), 2023
conté, charcoal, pastel, and acrylic on Mylar

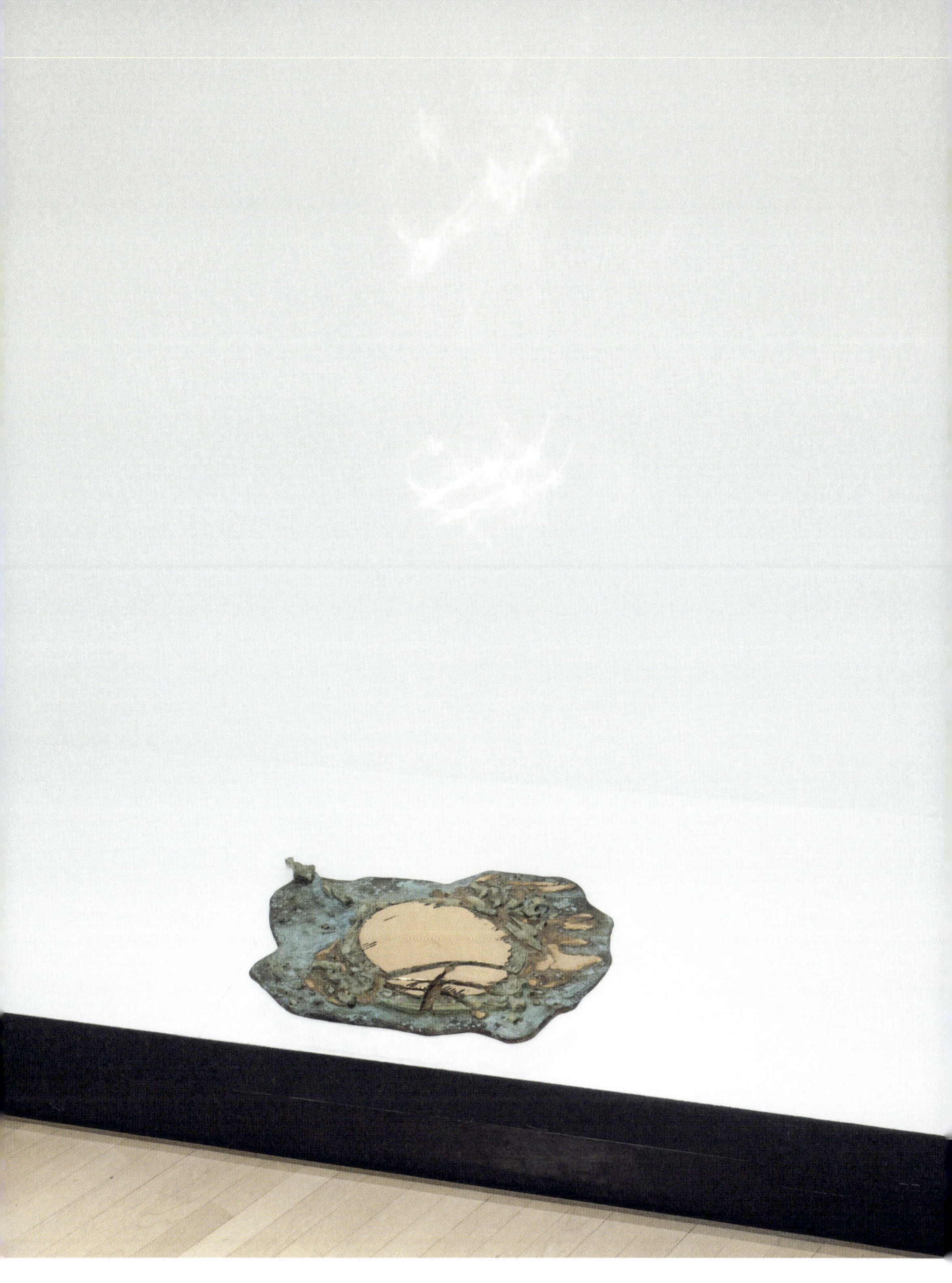

Untitled, 2014–21
bronze

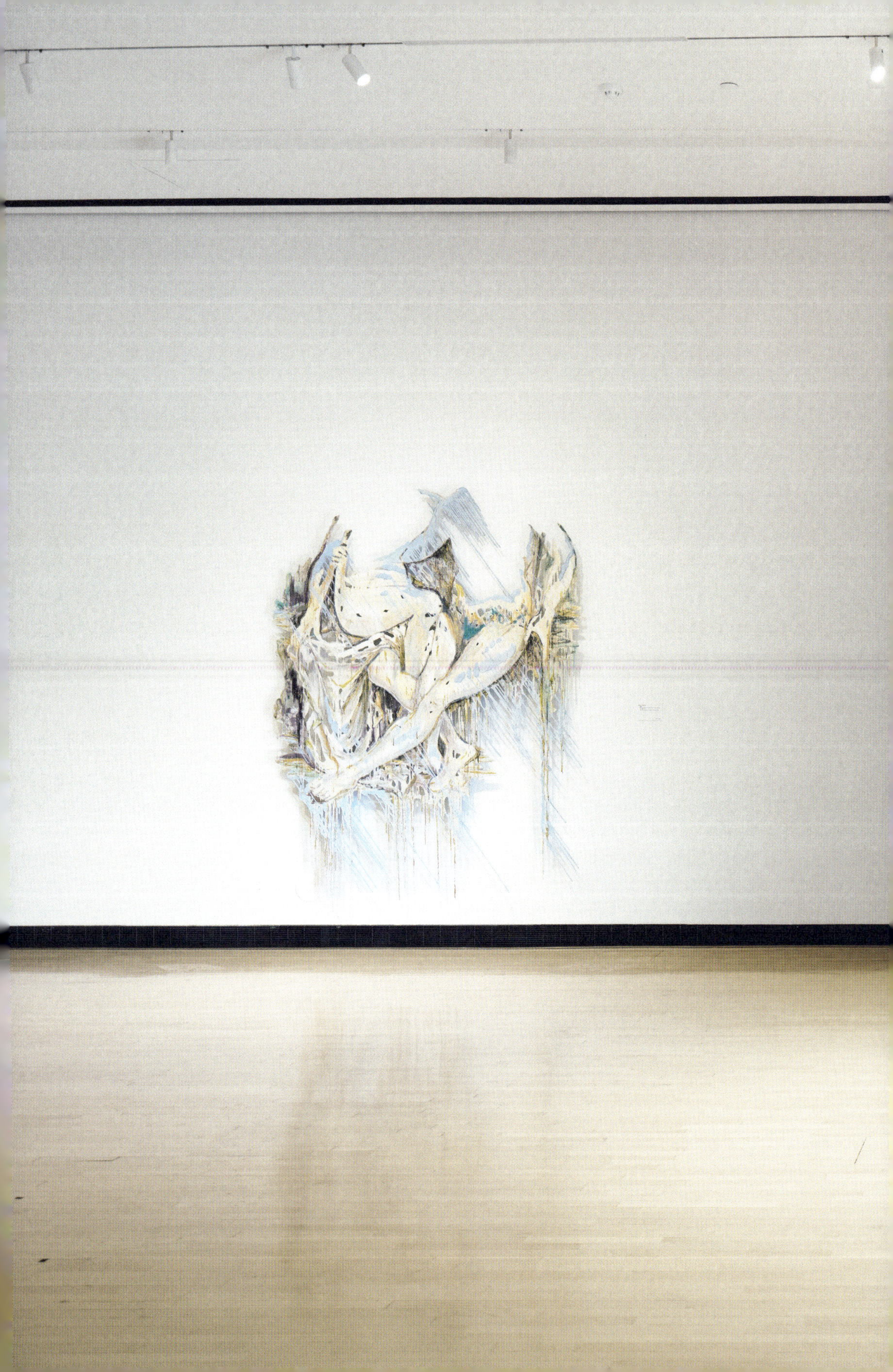

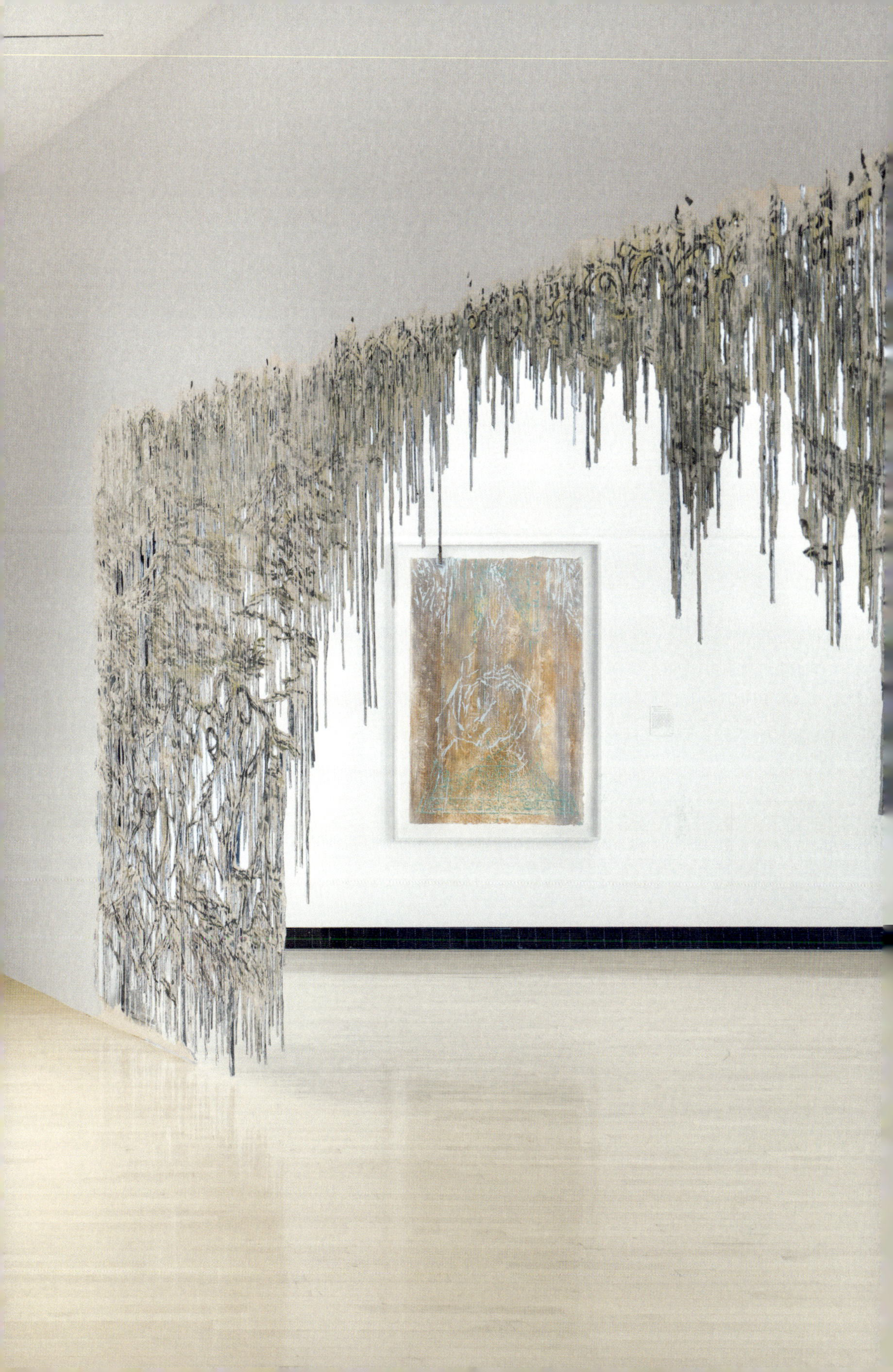

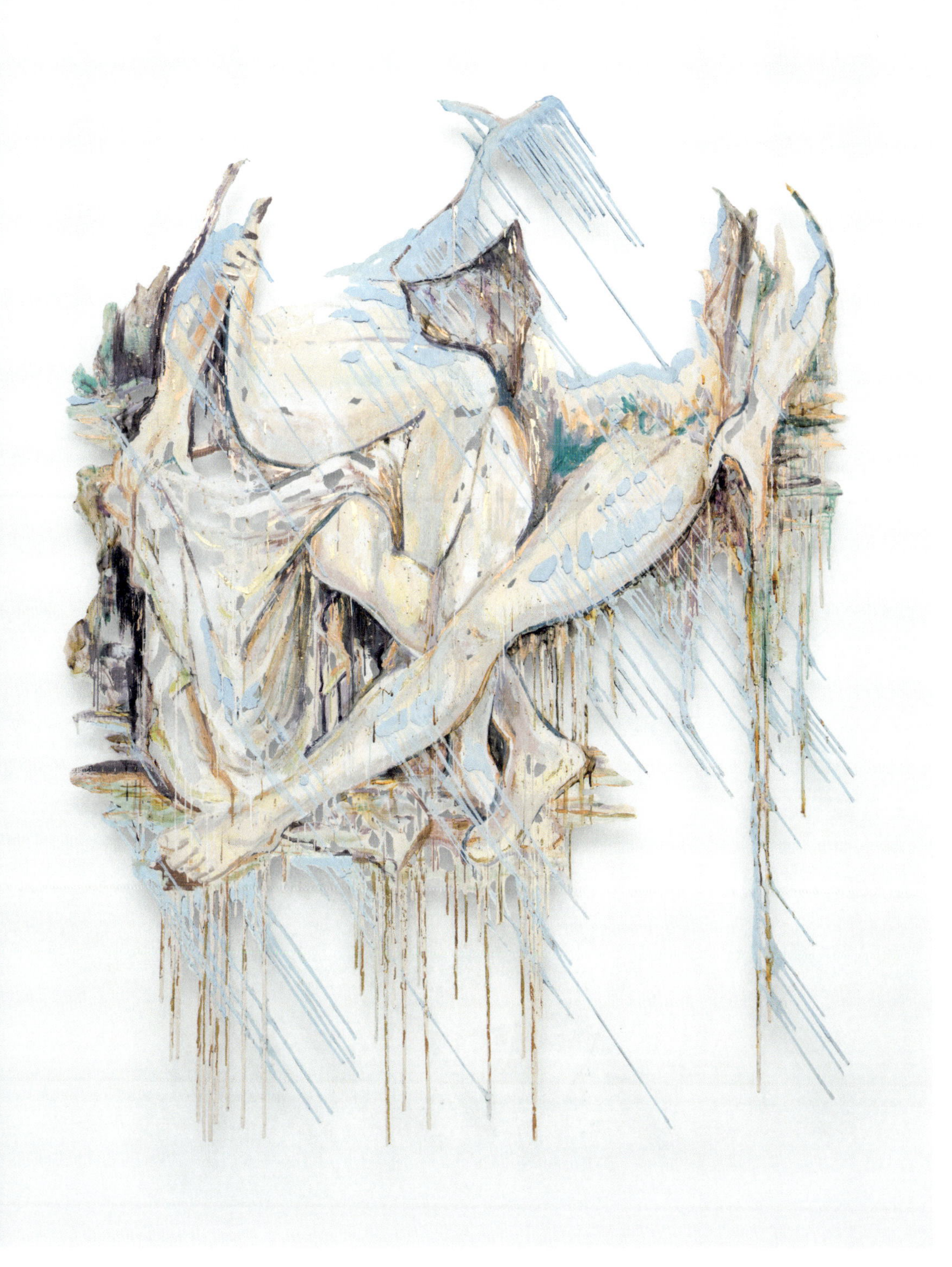

Mood: 11:14am, 2024
polymer gypsum, fiberglass, steel, plaster, metal leaf, and pigment

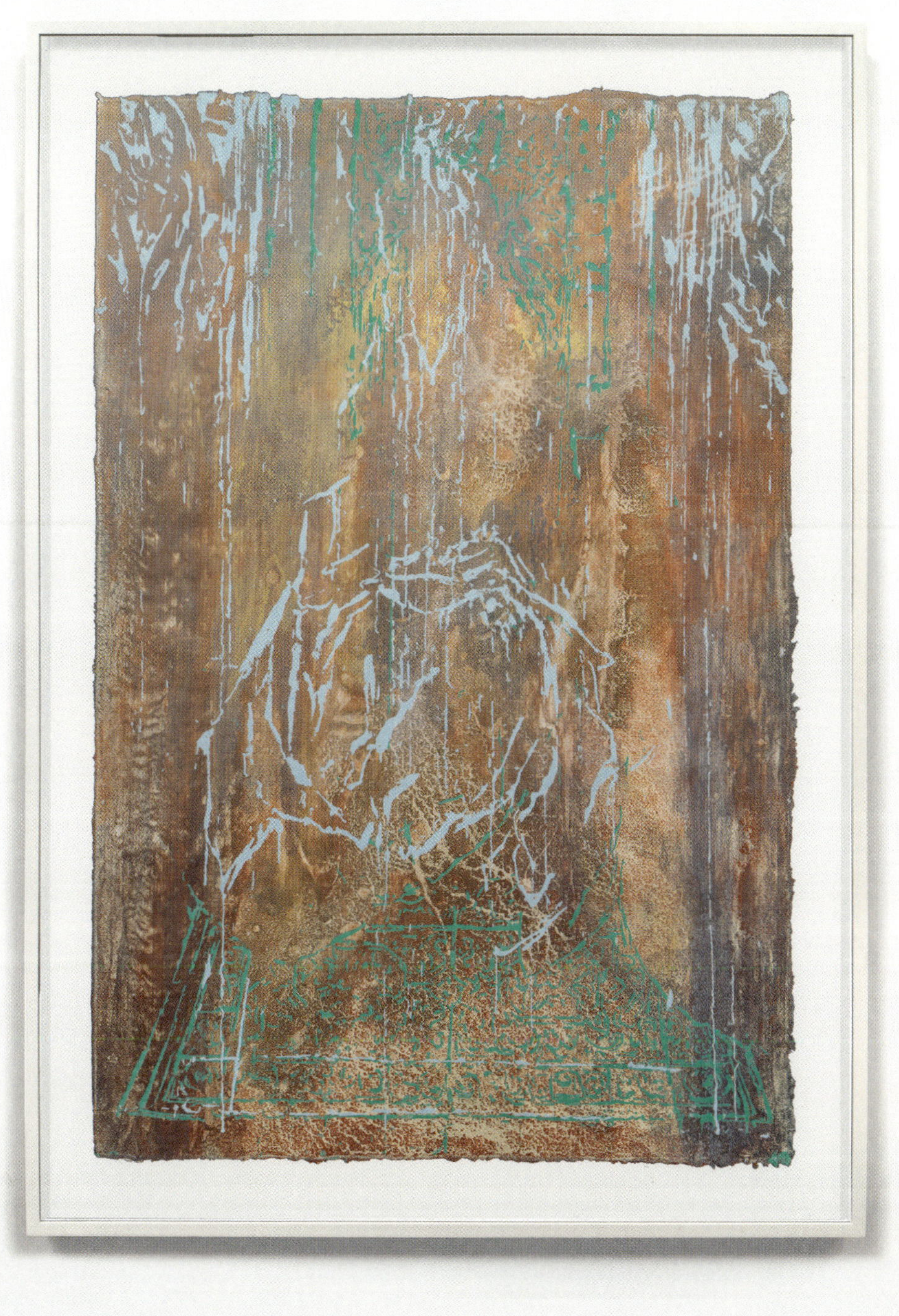

Mother in the Middle, 2023
linen pulp paint and cotton blowout on abaca base sheet

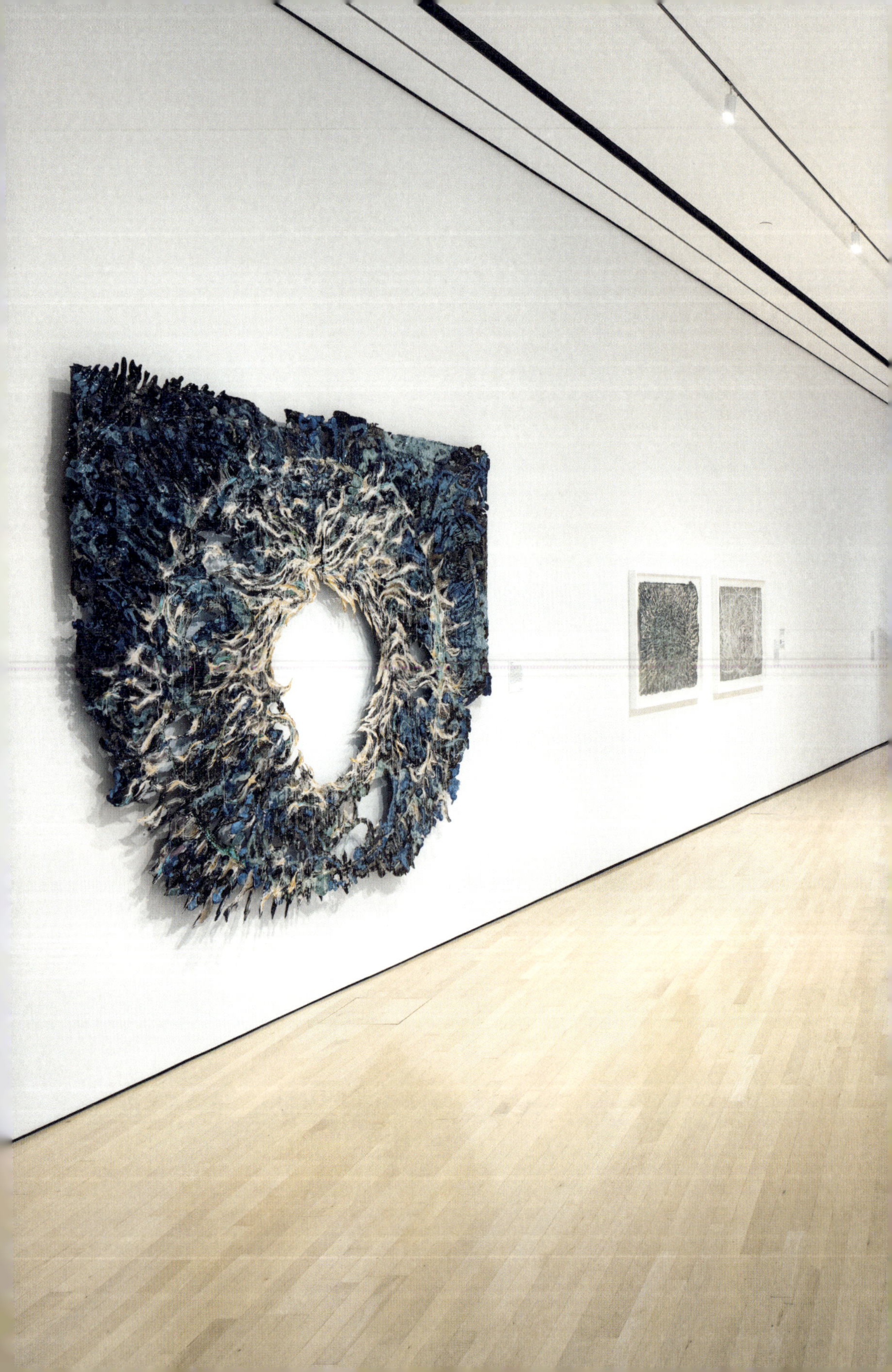

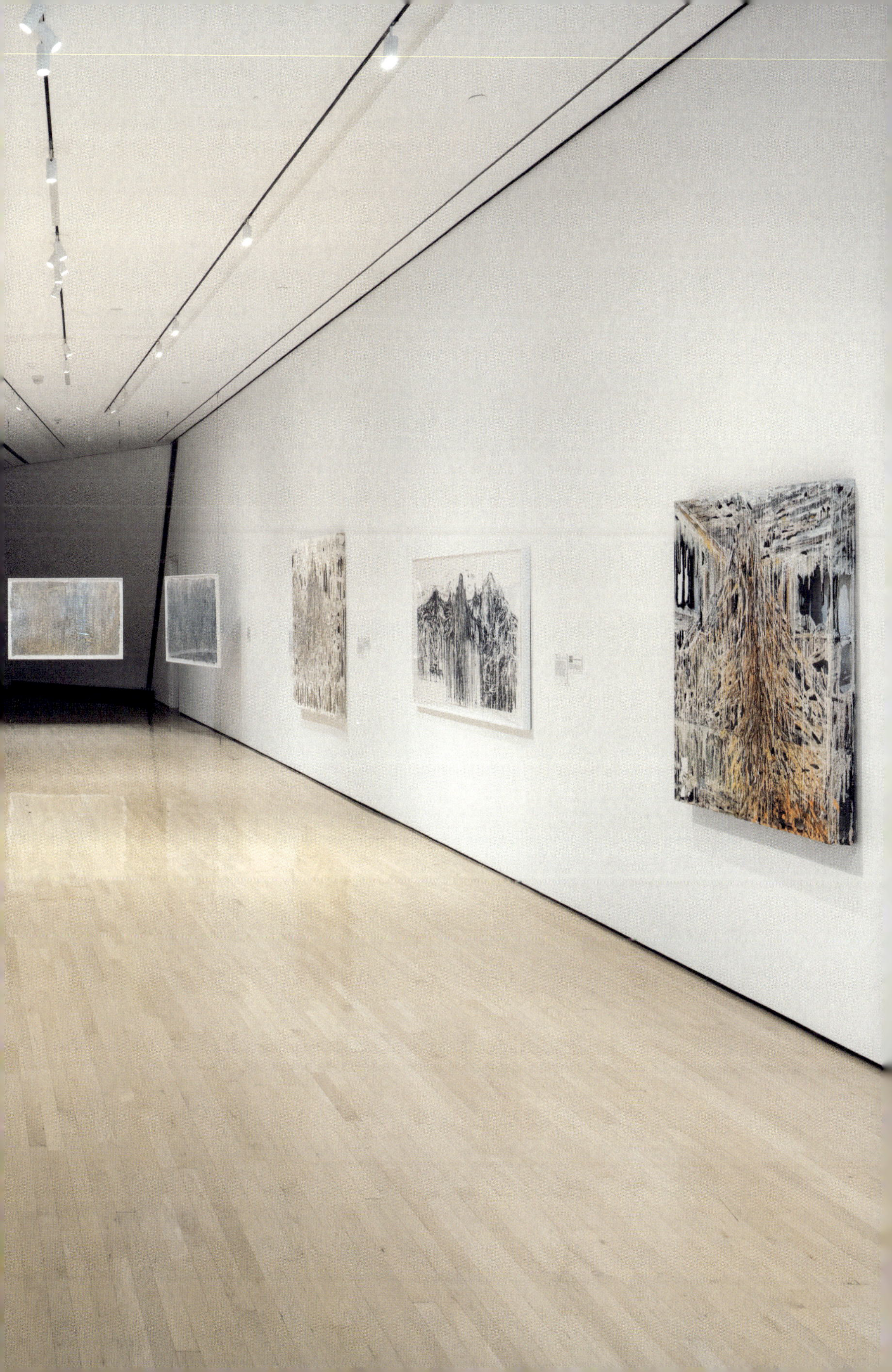

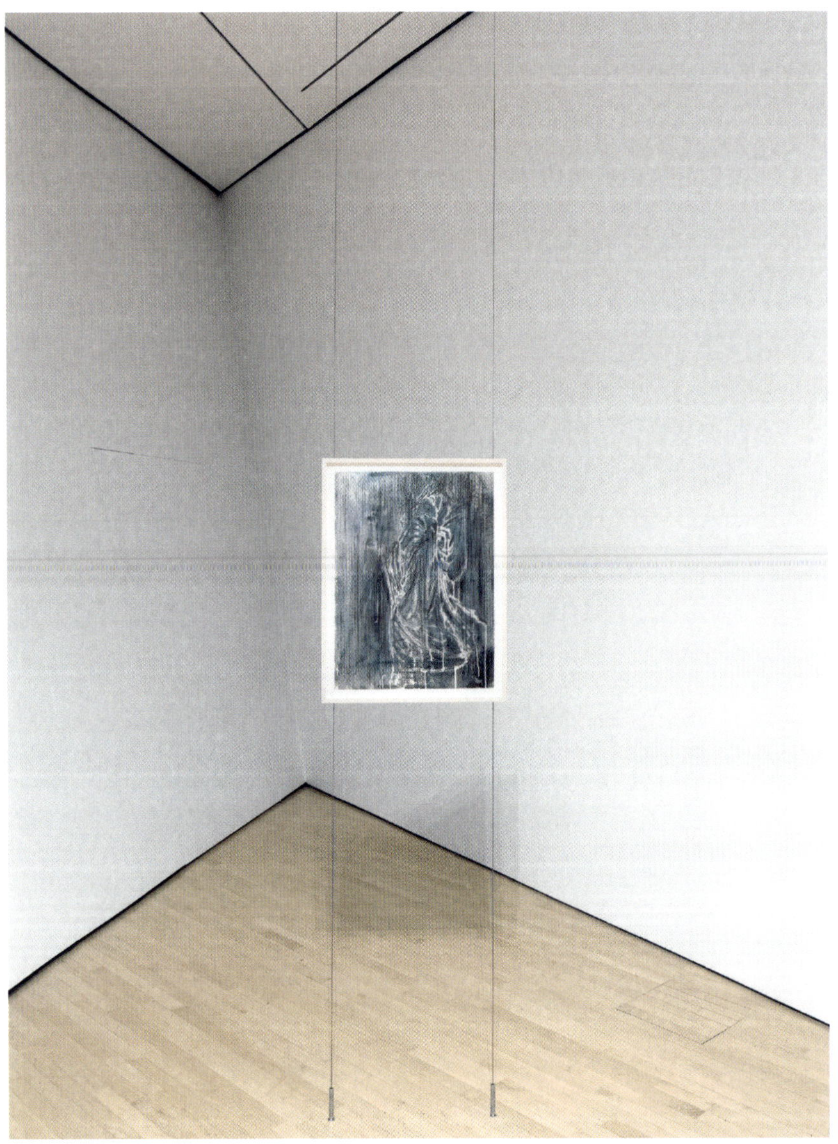

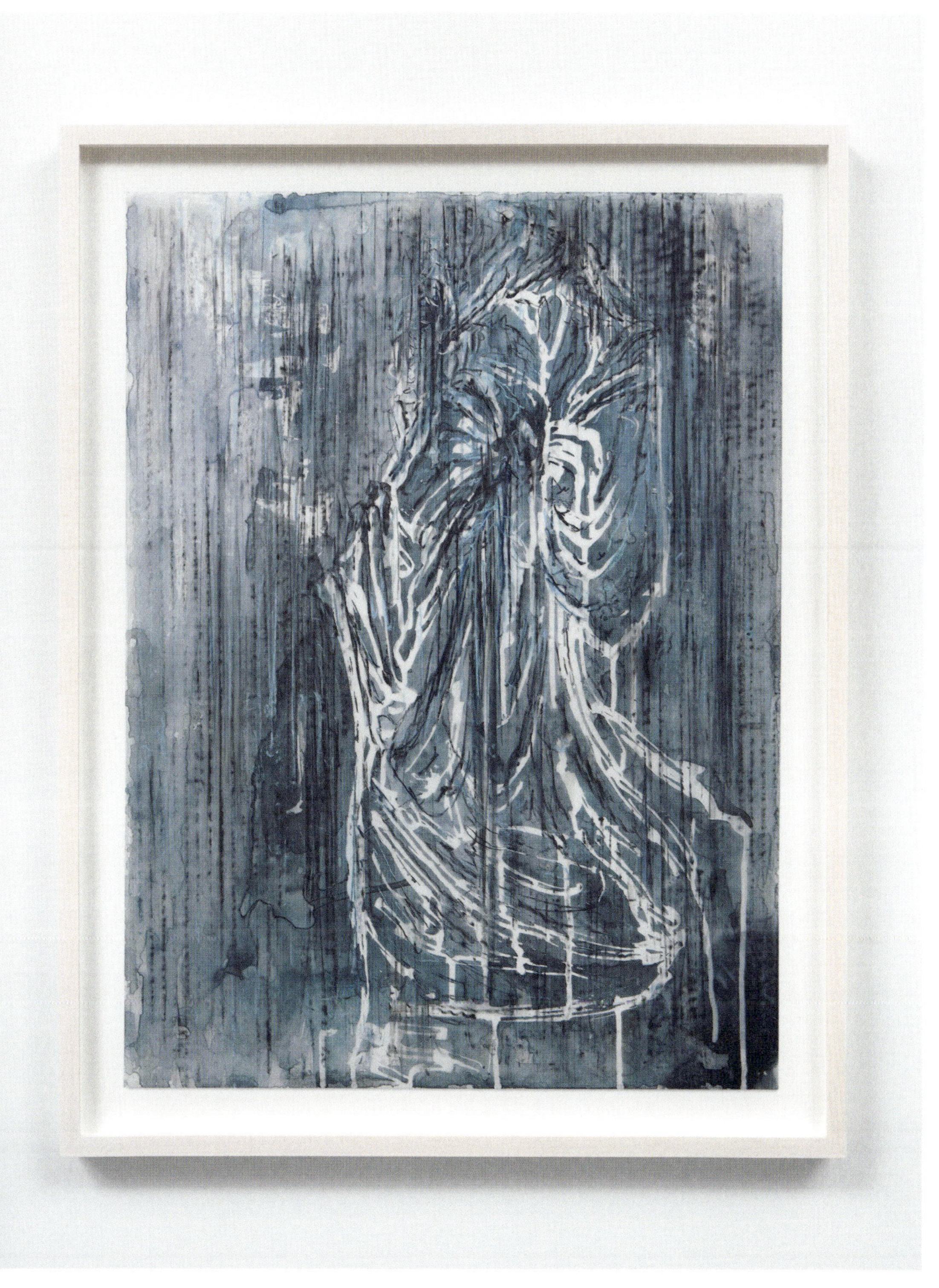

Untitled, 2013
conté, charcoal, pastel, and acrylic on Mylar

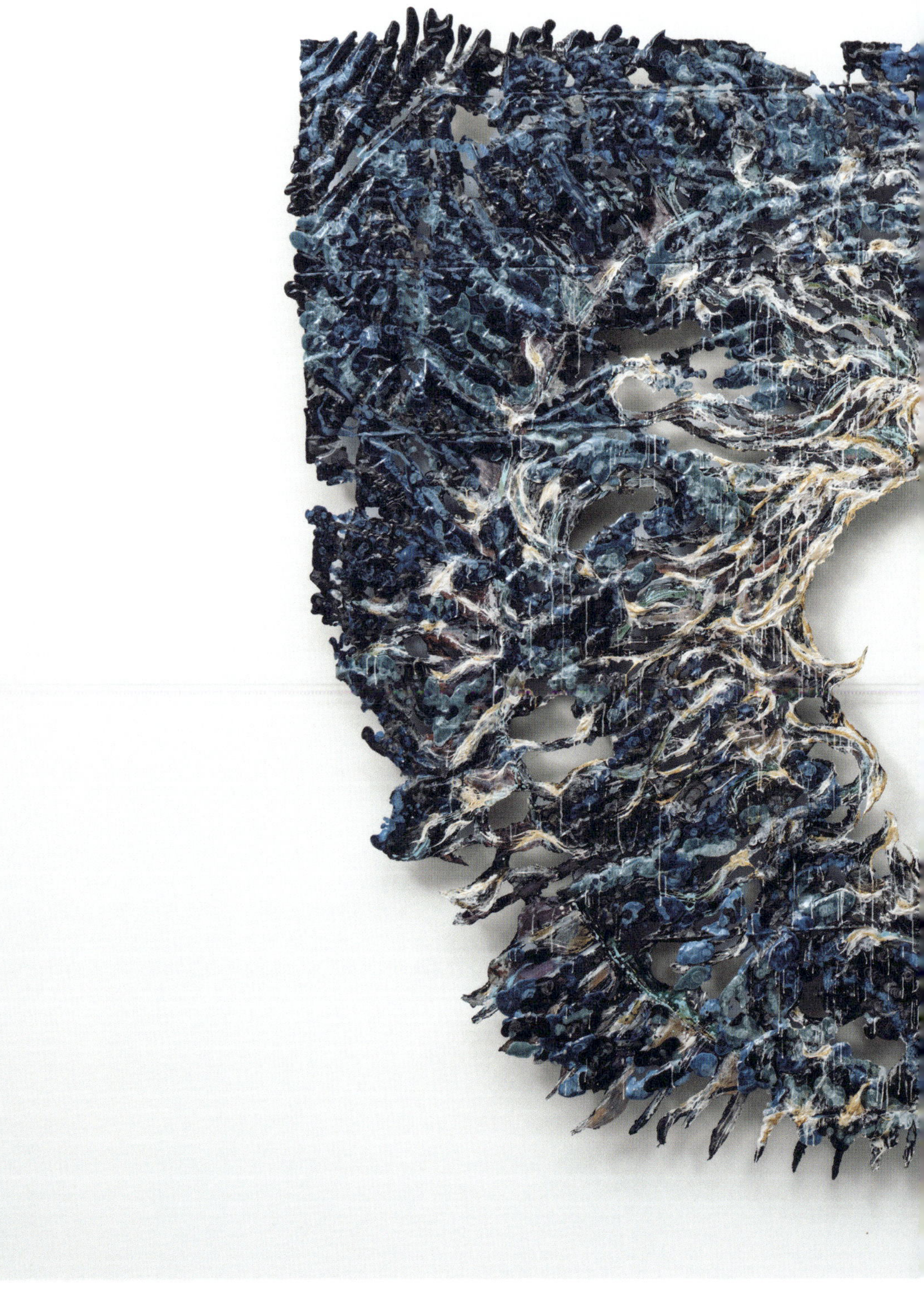

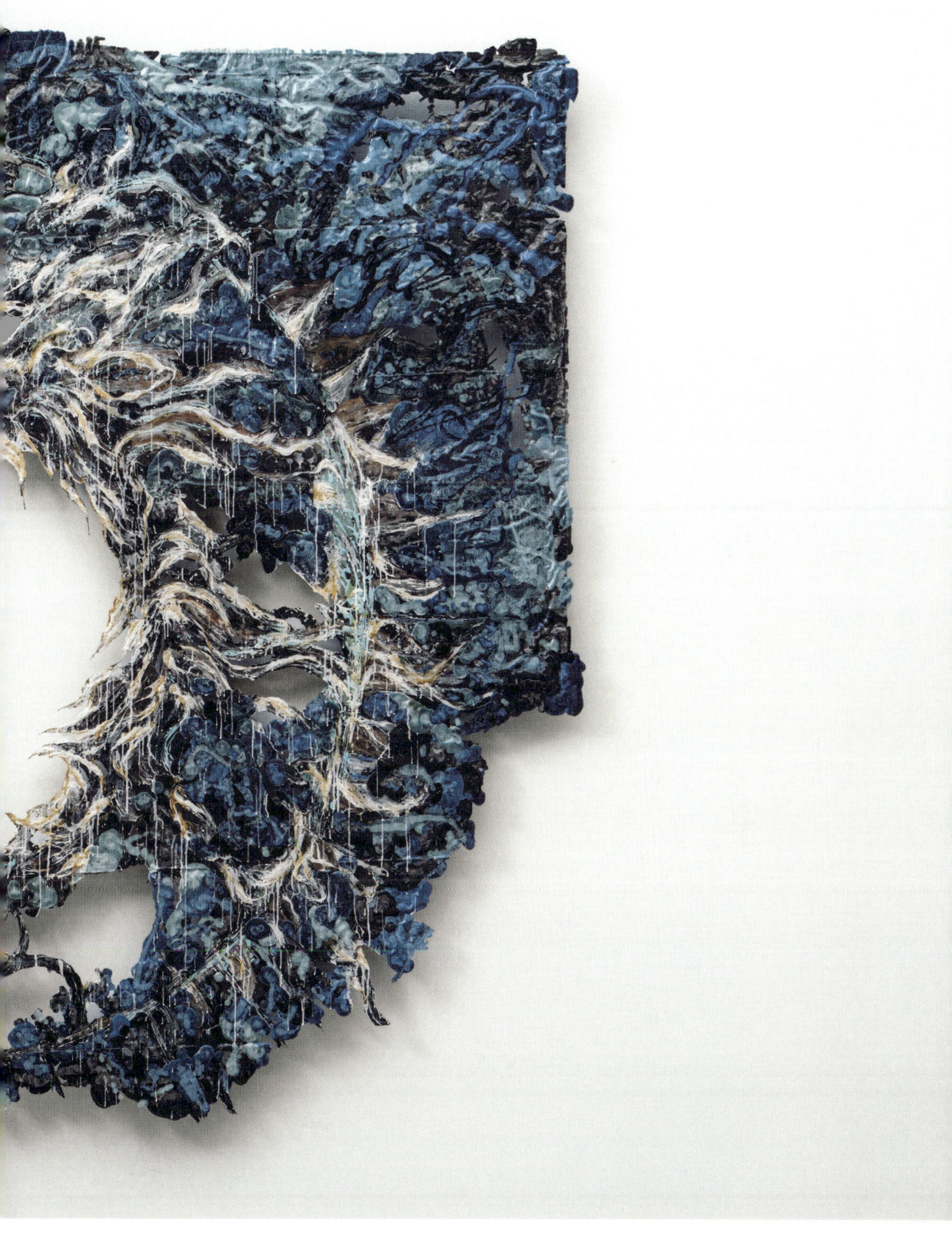

Blue Medusa, 2023
mixed media

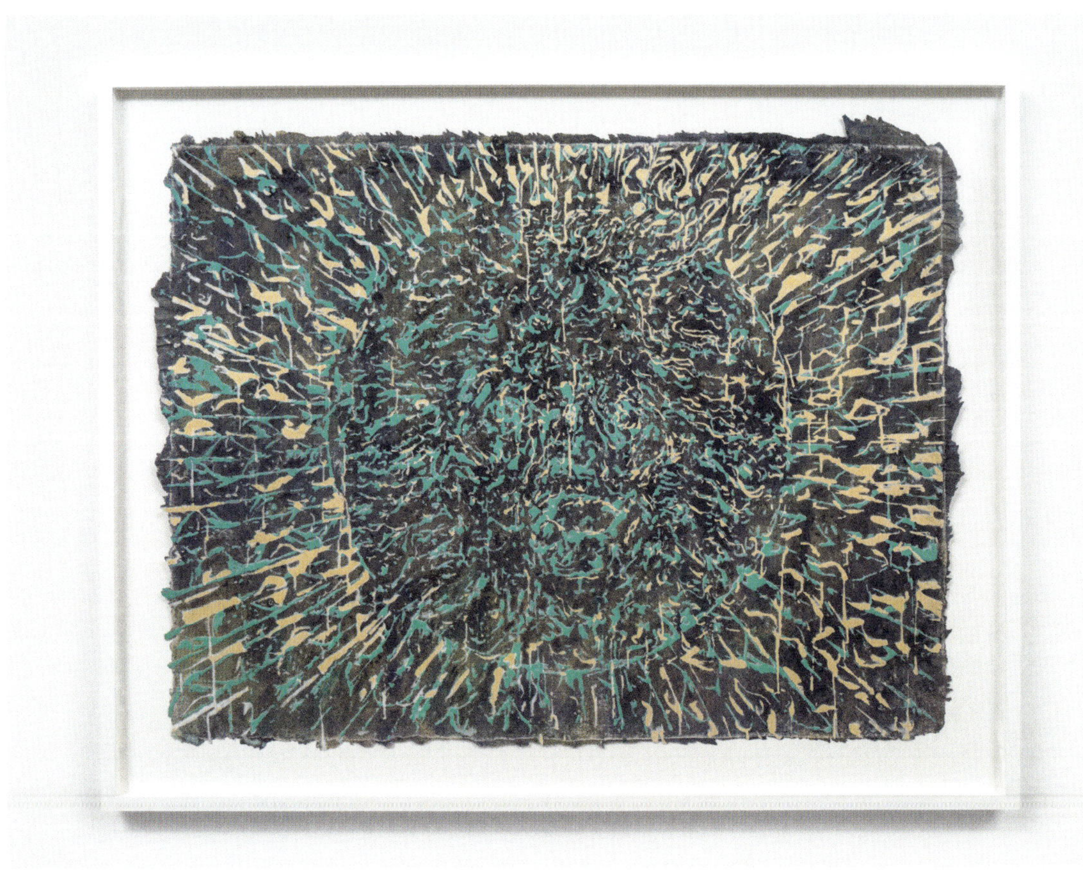

Night Medusa, 2023
linen pulp paint and cotton blowout on abaca base sheet

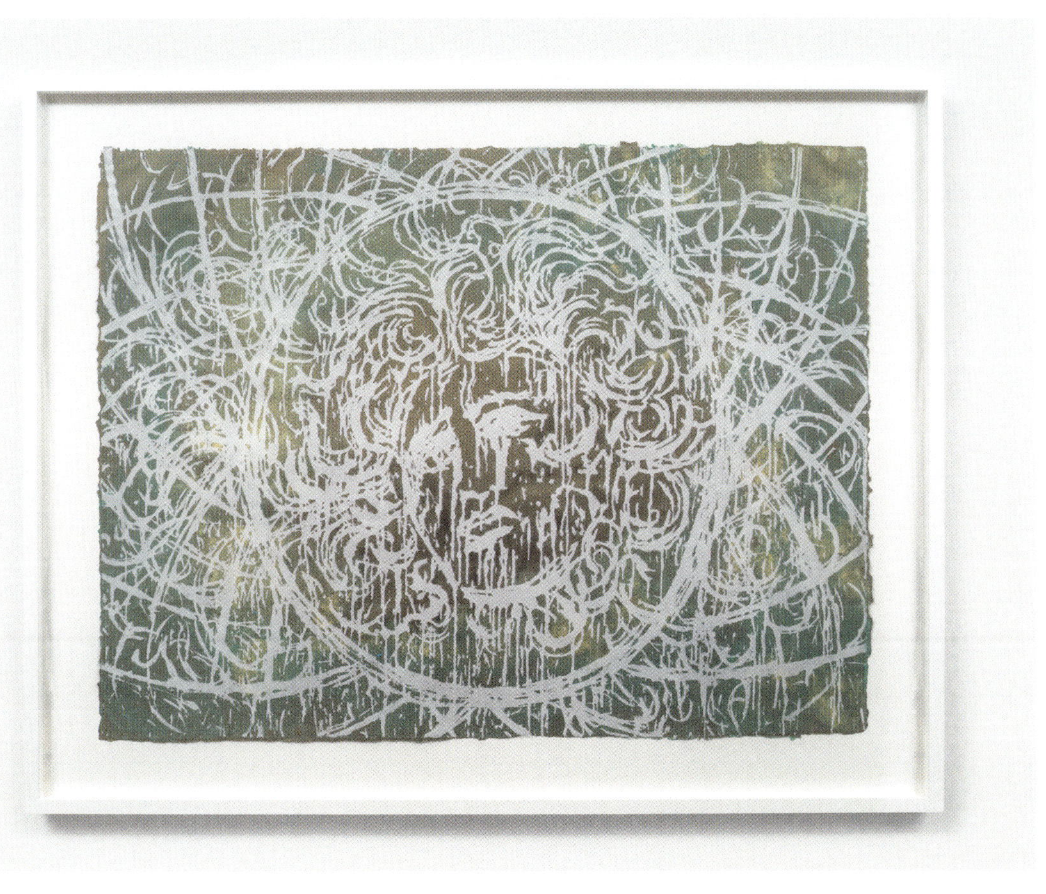

Mad Medusa, 2023
linen pulp paint and cotton blowout on abaca base sheet

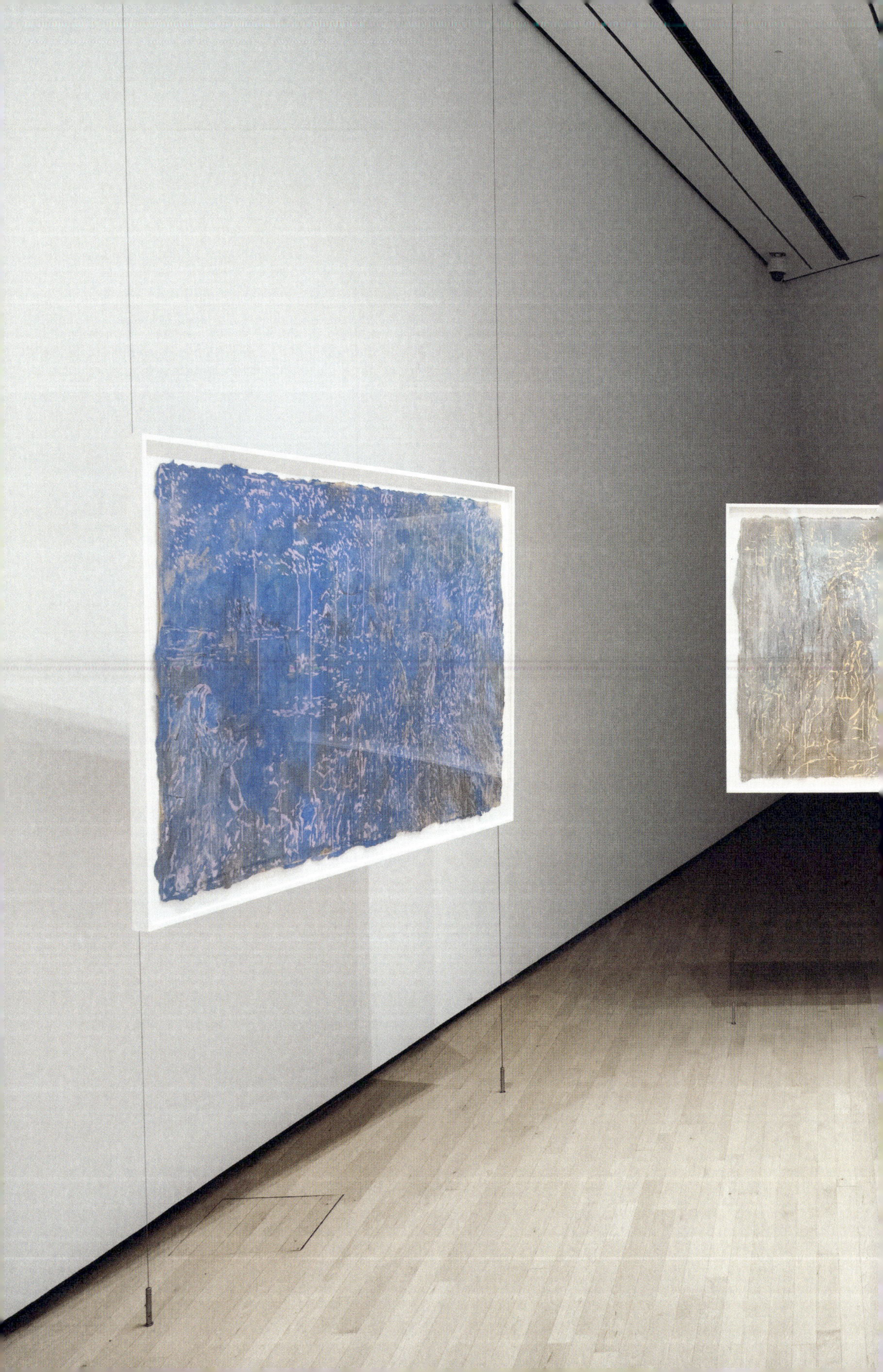

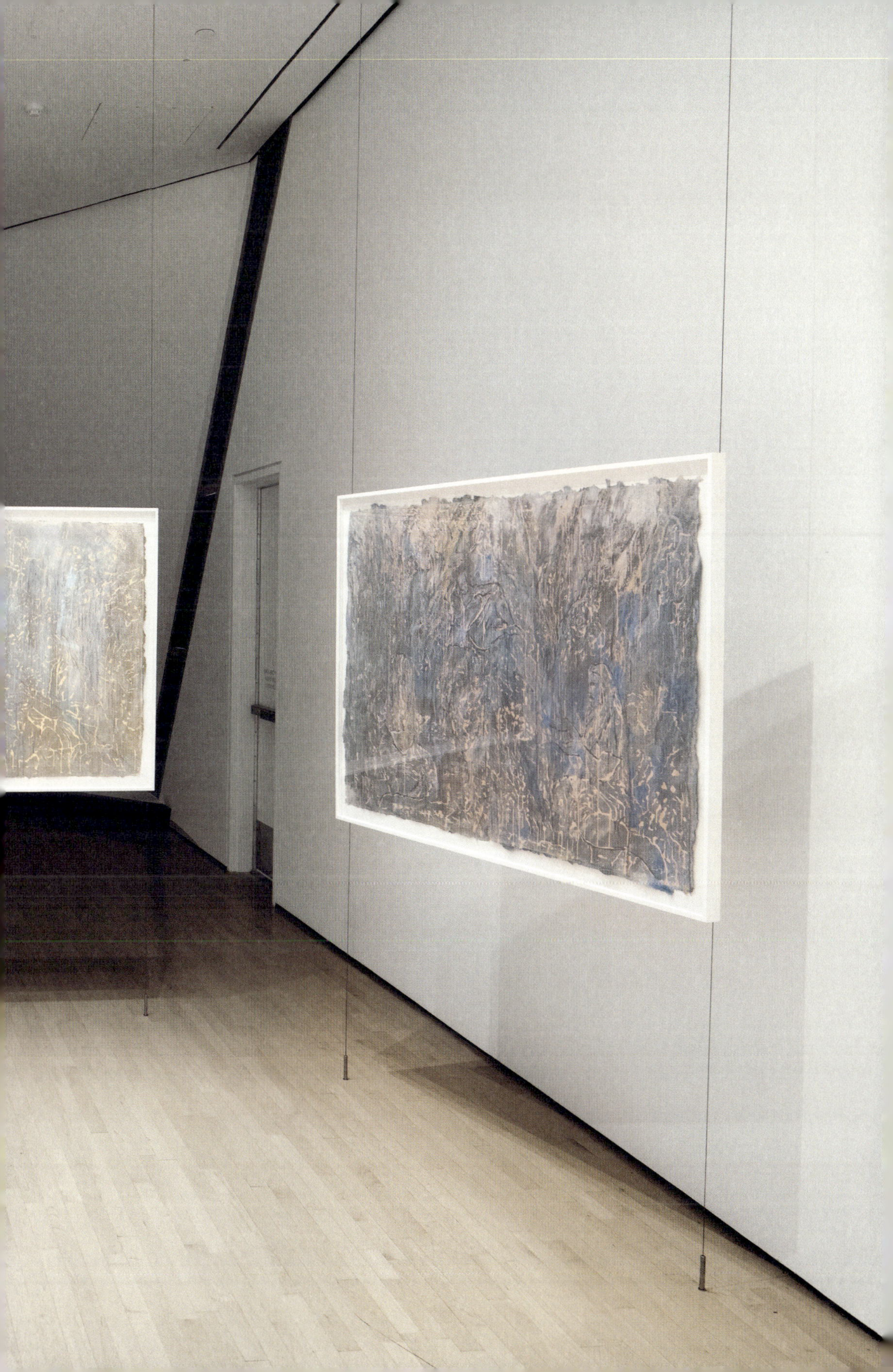

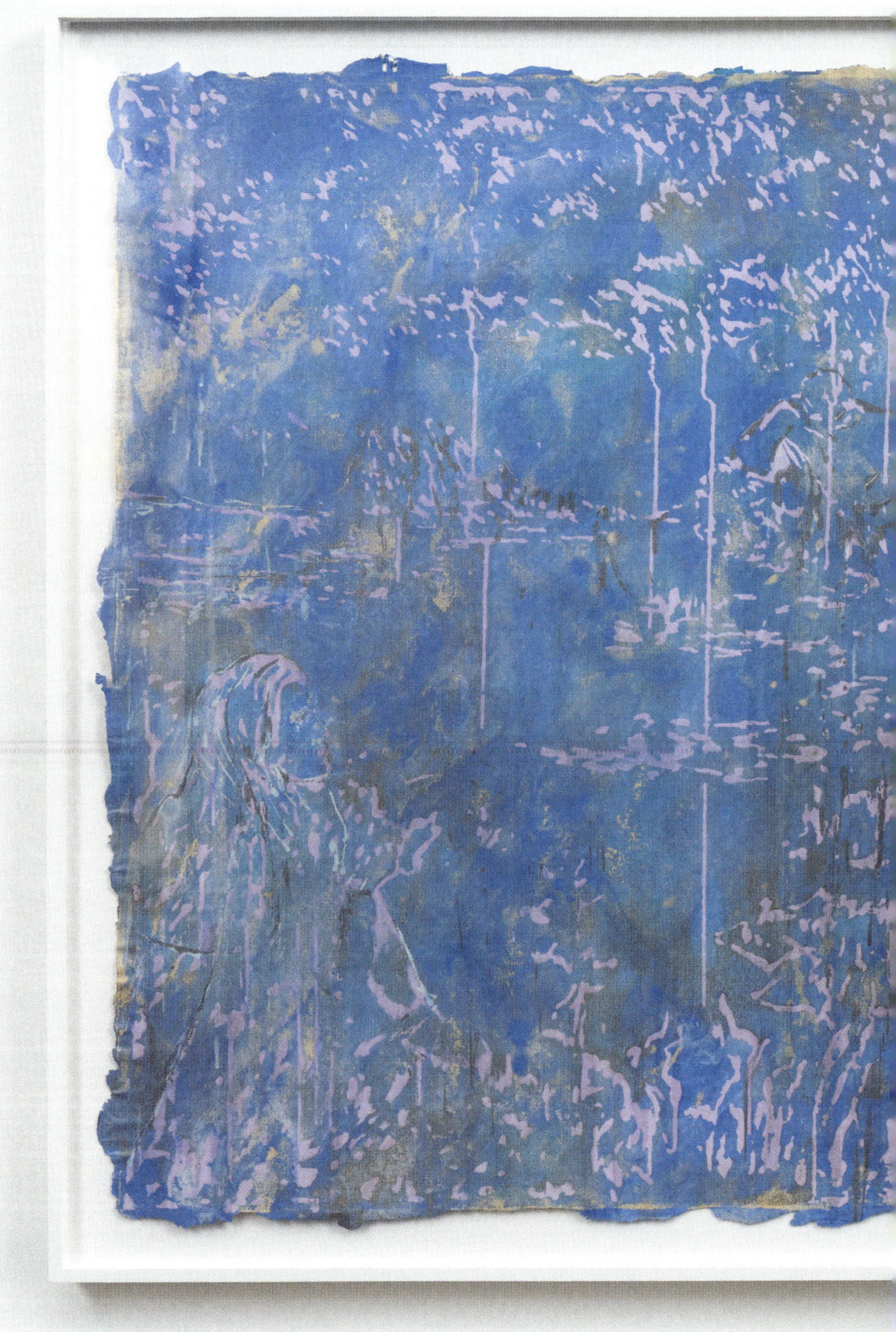

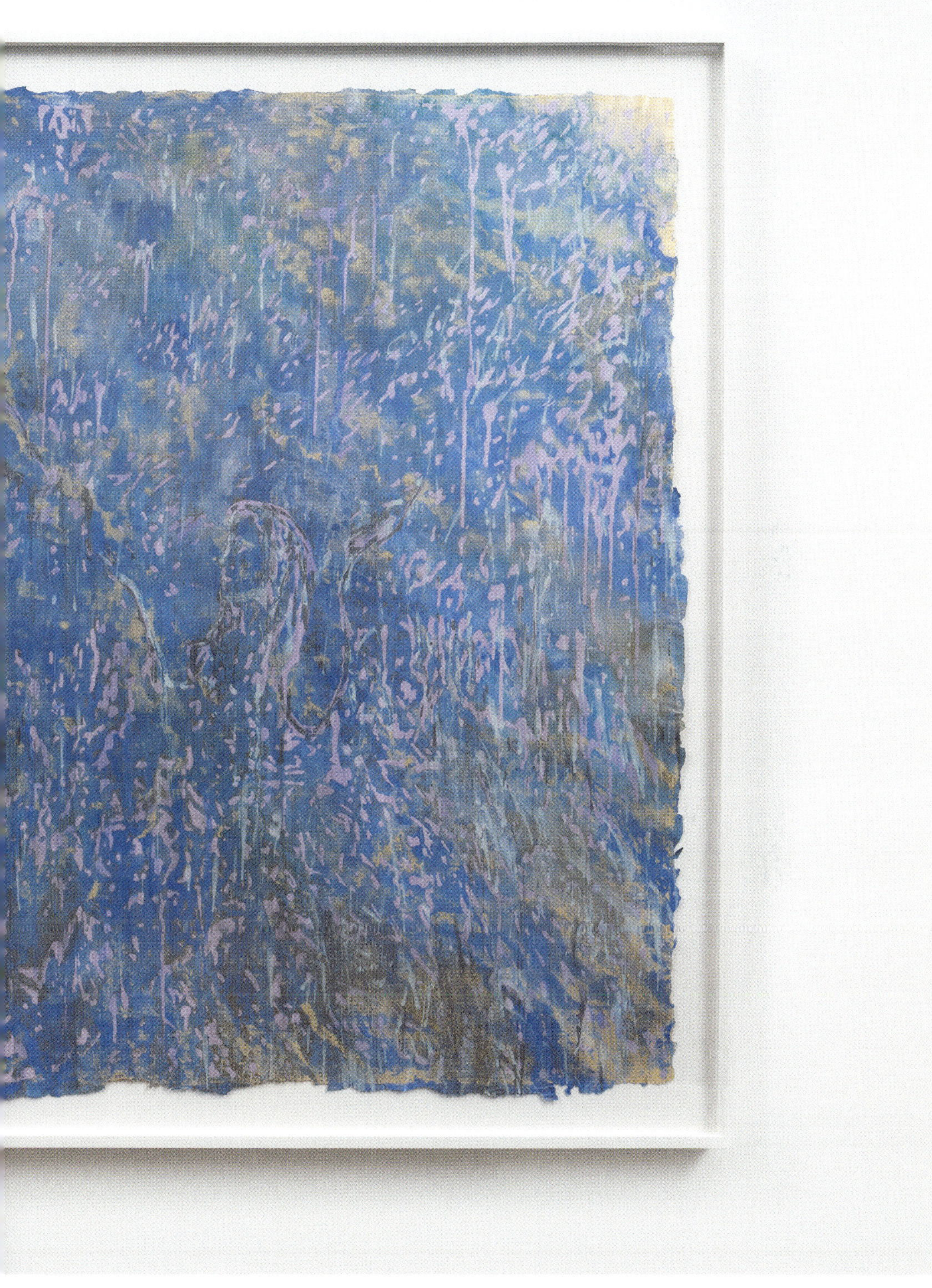

There was and there was not... two sisters who lived in the trees, 2025
linen pulp paint and cotton blowout on abaca base sheet

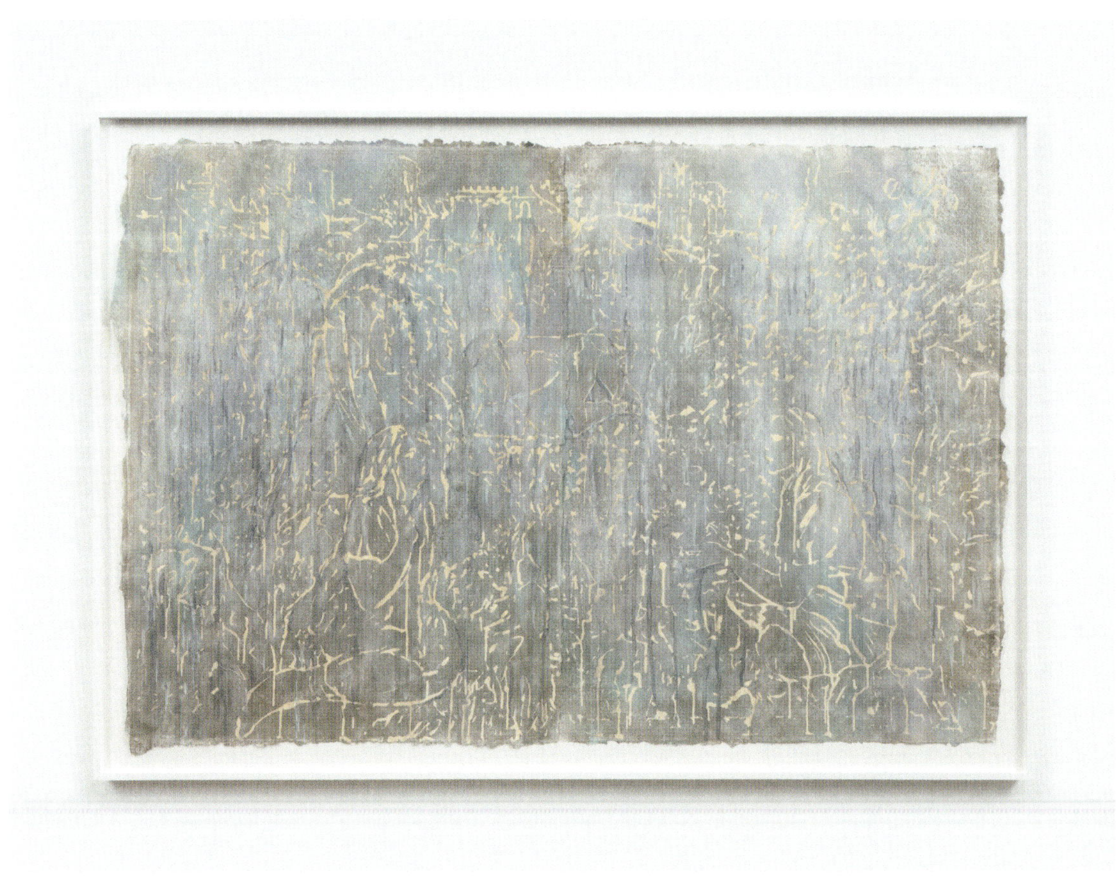

There was and there was not... a clever woman in disguise, 2025
linen pulp paint and cotton blowout on abaca base sheet

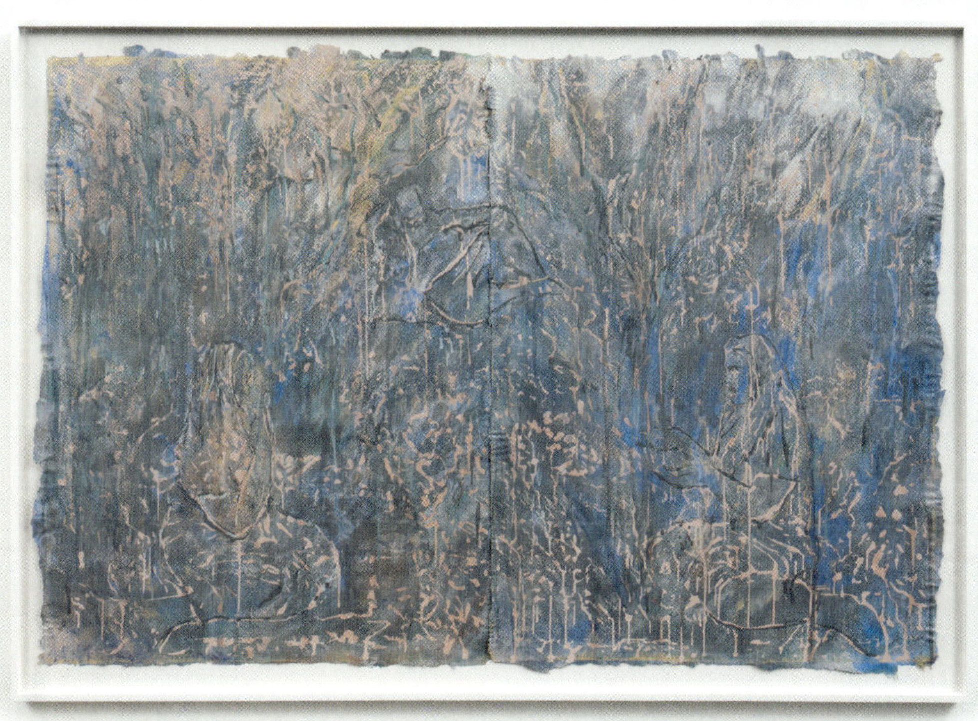

There was and there was not... a foolish king, 2025
linen pulp paint and cotton blowout on abaca base sheet

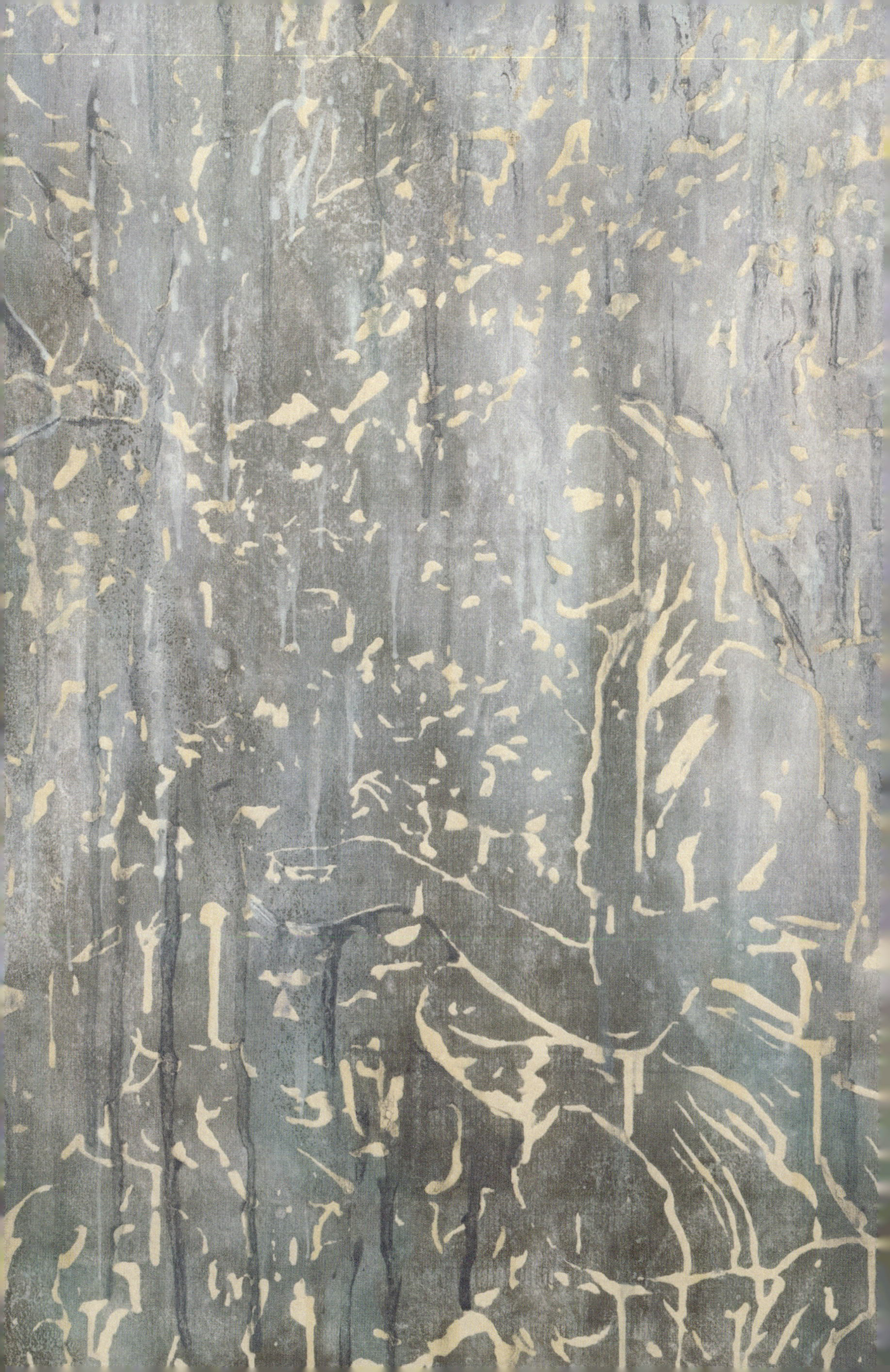

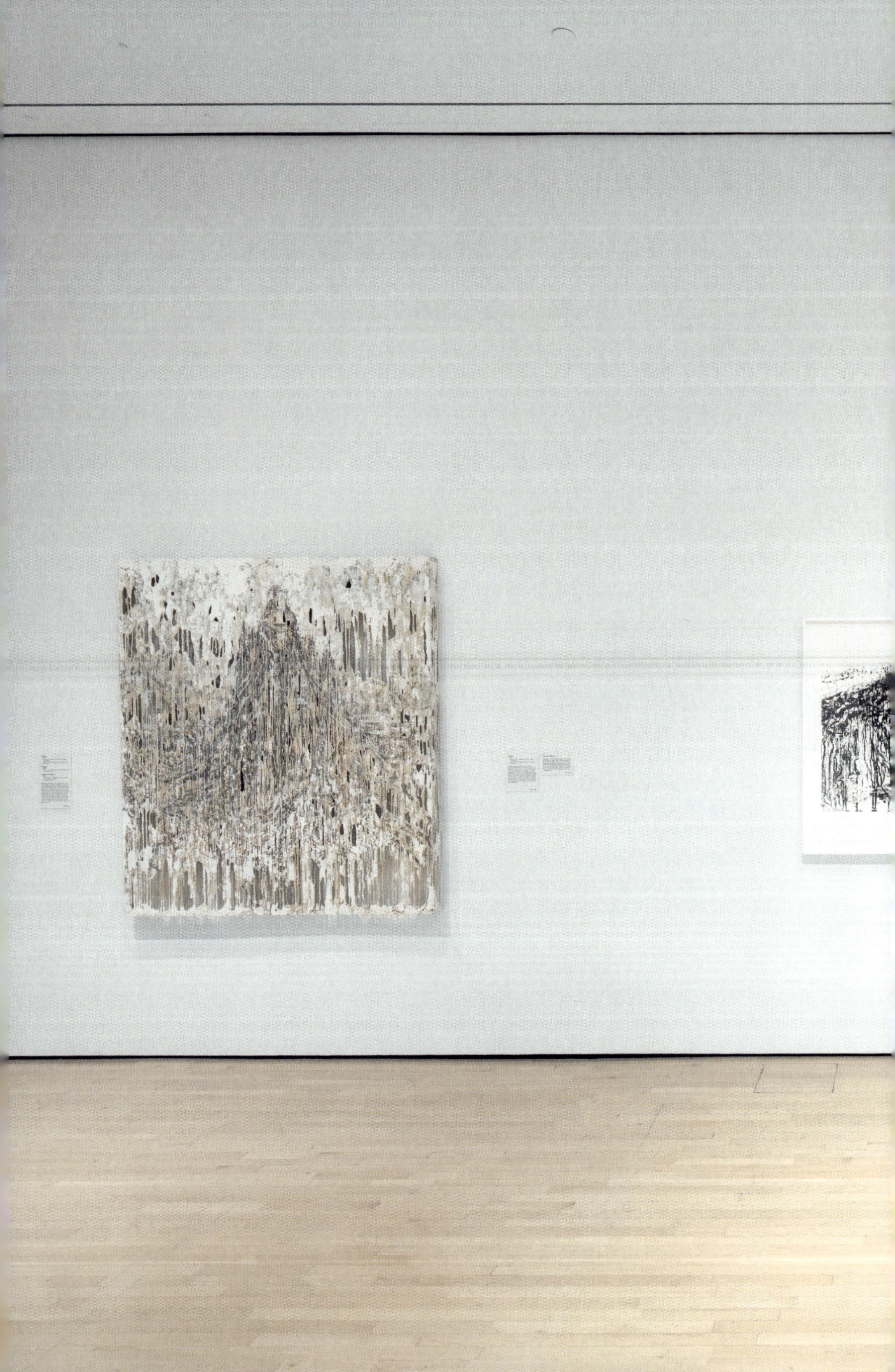

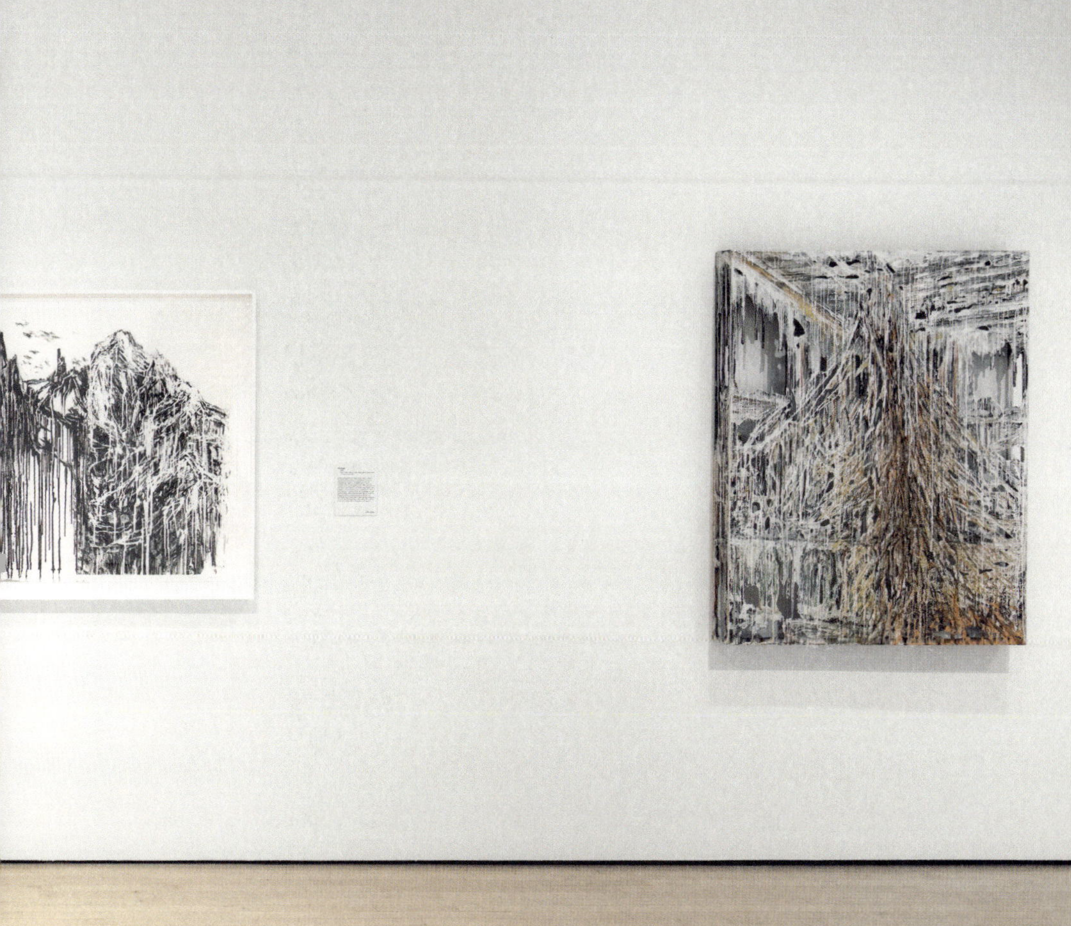

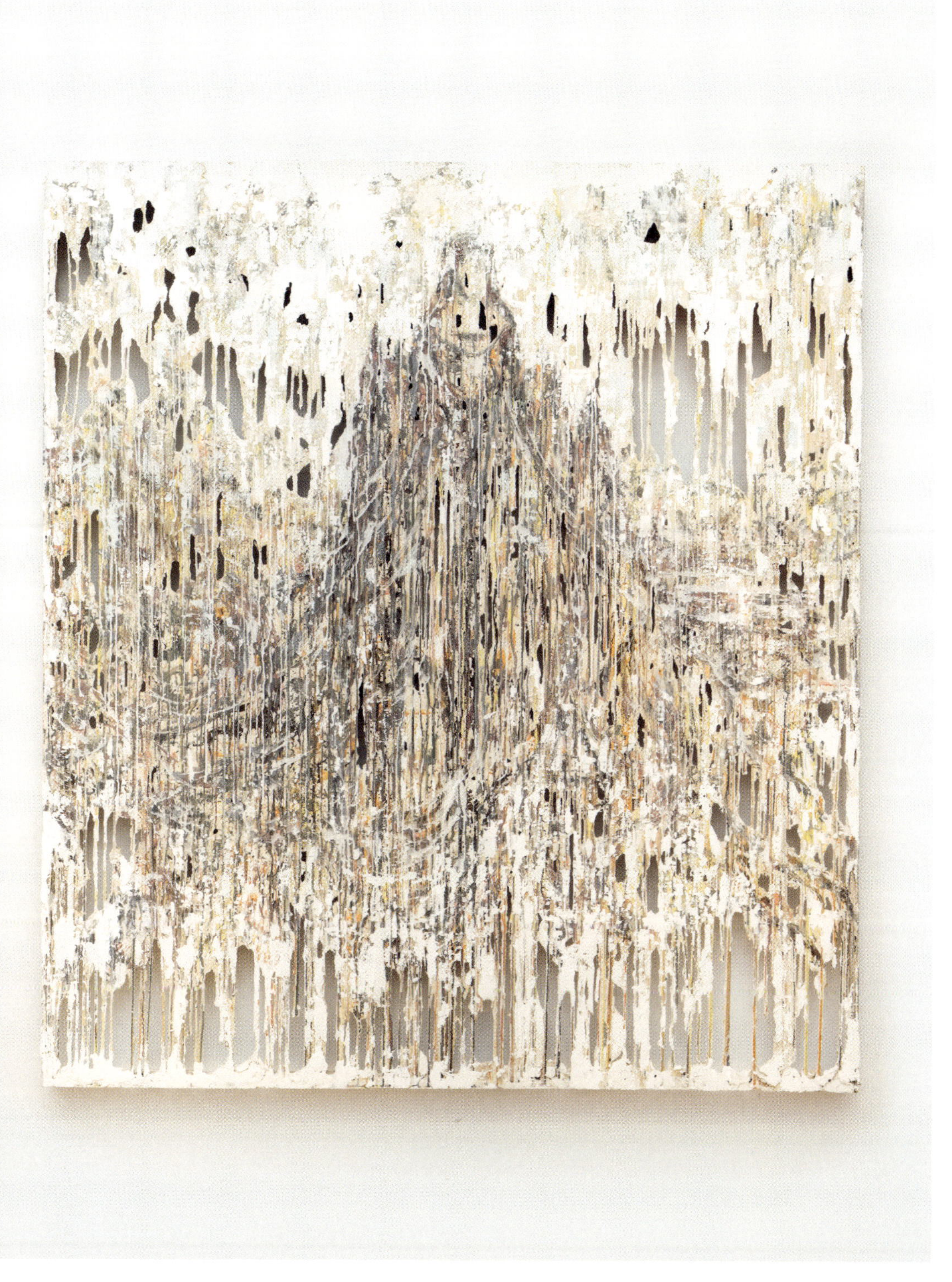

Lionless, 2013
polymer gypsum, fiberglass, steel, wood, plaster, and pigment

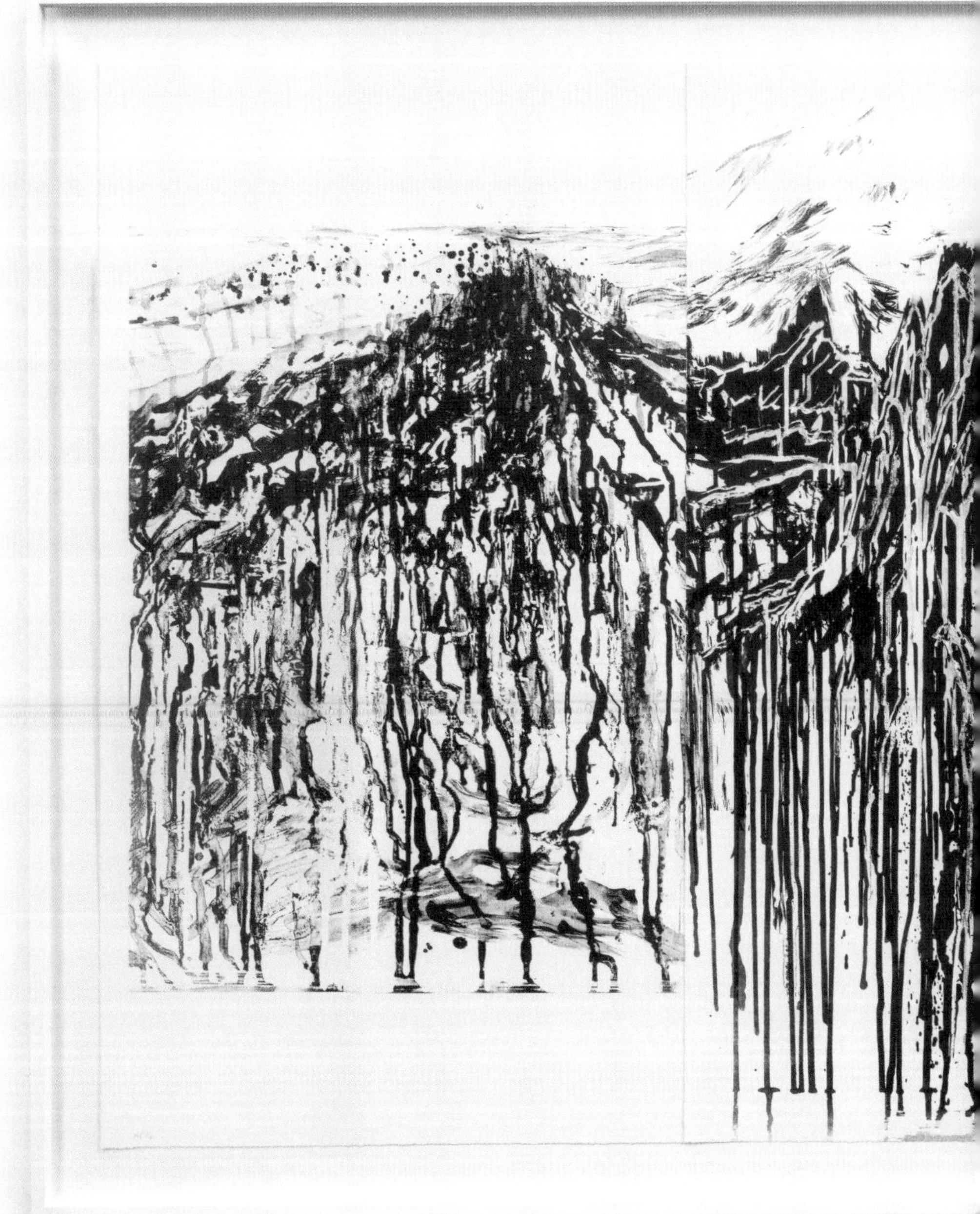

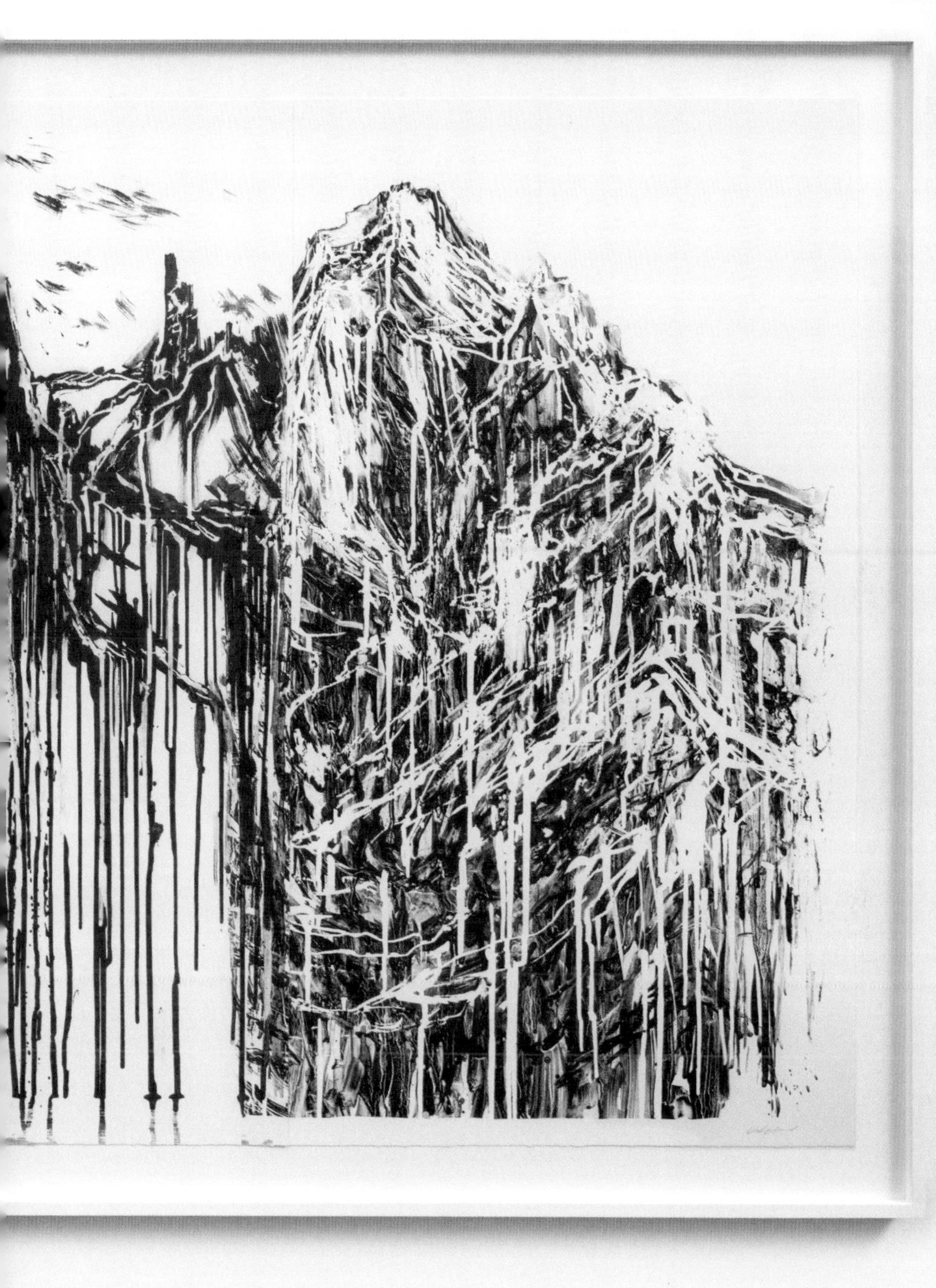

Hindsight, 2020
hand-drawn ballgrain plate lithograph on Essex paper
Edition of 20, plus 6 artist's proofs

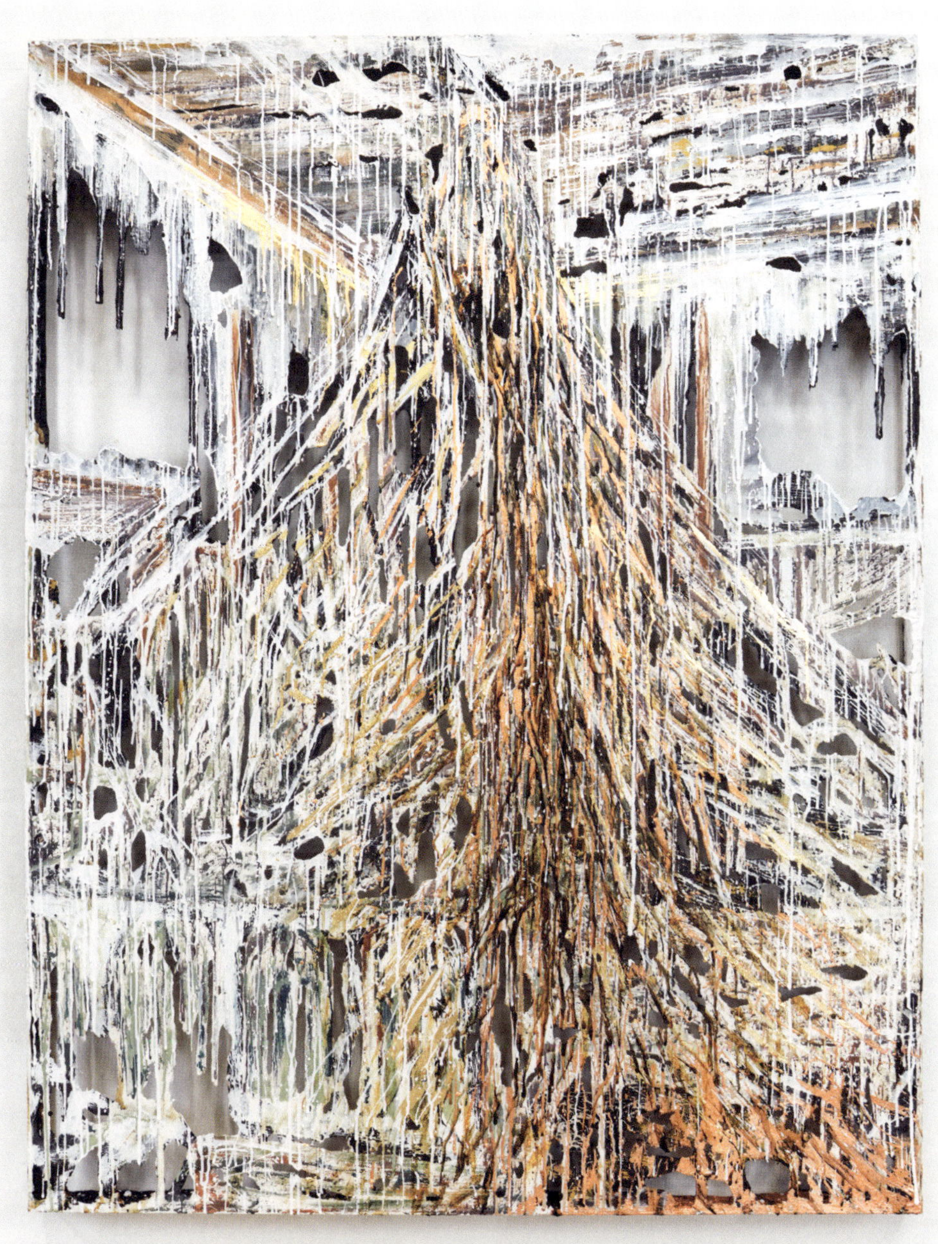

Deluge in the Allegory, 2020
polymer gypsum, fiberglass, steel, plaster, copper and gold leaf, and pigment

Various Possible Histories

Cassie Packard

‡
For more on the idea of prose architecture,
see: Renee Gladman, *Prose Architectures*
(Wave Books, 2017).

A masterwork of prose architecture, Italo Calvino's *Invisible Cities* (1972) unfolds as a conversation between Marco Polo and Kublai Khan, wherein the Venetian merchant-*cum*-travel writer regales the Mongol emperor with tales of dozens of fantastical cities he has encountered on his journeys.[1‡] He describes one metropolis composed entirely of visible plumbing; another whose cartography inexplicably corresponds to the design of a carpet of mysterious origins; a third perpetually haunted by its mirror image, a shadow self. Cities, he explains, are not built on logical premises but instead arise from a substrate of desires and fears. "You take delight not in a city's seven or seventy wonders, but in the answer it gives to a question of yours," Polo offers. "Or the question it asks you," responds Khan, "forcing you to answer, like Thebes through the mouth of the Sphinx."[2]

Diana Al-Hadid's beguiling structures are likewise psychogeographic and poetic, akin to a city's question ventriloquized by a chimera. An architect of the imaginary, she creates towers, screens, cathedrals, fountains, and monuments that are dense yet permeable: variously honeycombed and latticed, porous and fibrillar. Gravitationally implausible or perspectivally askew, the artist's teeming, toppling structures recall buildings in dreams. They also evoke the surreal edifices and cityscapes found in such historic works as Giovanni Battista Piranesi's *Prima Parte di Architetture, e Prospettive* (1743) (fig. 1), a series of etchings featuring spatially ambiguous and functionally unbuildable architectures inspired by ancient ruins, or Pieter Bruegel the Elder's *The Tower of Babel* (c. 1563) (fig. 2), an oil-on-panel painting based on the biblical parable about the loss of a common language and a spiraling tower left unfinished. (Al-Hadid cites both artists as part of the sprawling yet specific map of her thinking.) Across her freestanding sculptures, panel paintings, and works on paper, Al-Hadid explores myths of place and myth as a place. She repeatedly returns to the worldbuilding capacity of stories—particularly those that have accreted, transformed, and splintered in both the transition from oral to written transmission and across generations of translation and reinterpretation.

Born in Aleppo, Syria, in 1981, Al-Hadid immigrated with her family to Canton, Ohio, when she was five years old. She grew up, as she puts it, a "third culture kid."[3] With an emphasis on finely detailed works in Western and Islamic art history, her constellation of references runs the gamut: from Northern Renaissance paintings that promote chastity to Falnama illustrations used to predict the future, from water clocks by a Mesopotamian artist-engineer to an ancient Greek relief that Sigmund Freud displayed in replica in his study (see p. 17). These touchstones don't only draw from disparate time periods and geocultural contexts; they also underscore cultural cross-pollination and convergence, evident in her interest in the figure of Scheherazade, whom she characterizes as "running against the grain of how the West conceives of women in the Middle East."[4] A skilled storyteller contending with high stakes, Scheherazade is the unreliable narrator of *One Thousand and One Nights*. These nested, labyrinthine folktales of Persian, Arabic, and Indian origin are traceable to the 9th century but were first collected as a French translation in the 18th century; they have continued to grow and shapeshift with time, influencing a litany of writers including Calvino, Georges Perec, and Jorge Luis Borges.

After completing an undergraduate degree in art and art history at Kent State University, Al-Hadid studied sculpture at Virginia Commonwealth University in Richmond, graduating from the MFA program in 2005. "I didn't want to make things," she recalls. "I wanted to make places. I wanted to make whole environments."[5] In her graduate thesis, which was informed by research into theories of place, topology, and ornament, she wrote: "My places are impossible places. They are irregular, illogical, and unstable… The irrational is always an option, a lingering threat."[6] One year later, she produced what would come to be known as her breakout work, and the earliest

pp. 4, 13, 29, 30, 32–33 piece in *unbecoming*. *Spun of the Limits of my Lonely Waltz* (2006) looks to the 1680s, when, at the behest of Louis XIV, French choreographer

fig. 1 Giovanni Battista Piranesi, *Prima Parte di Architetture, e Prospettive (First Edition, Third Issue)*, dated 1743 but printed 1747.

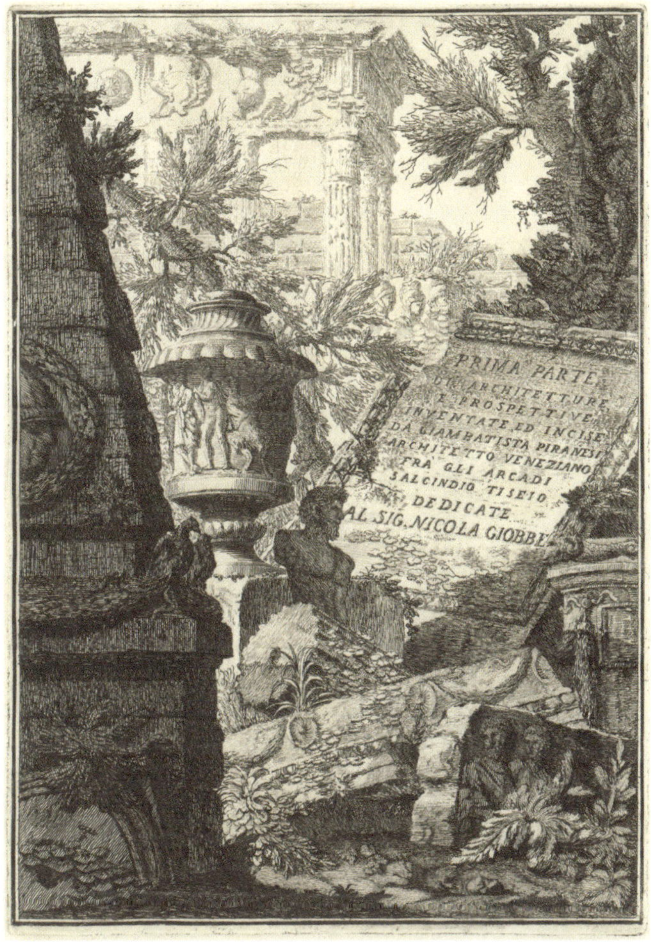

fig. 2 Pieter Bruegel the Elder, *The Tower of Babel*, c. 1563.

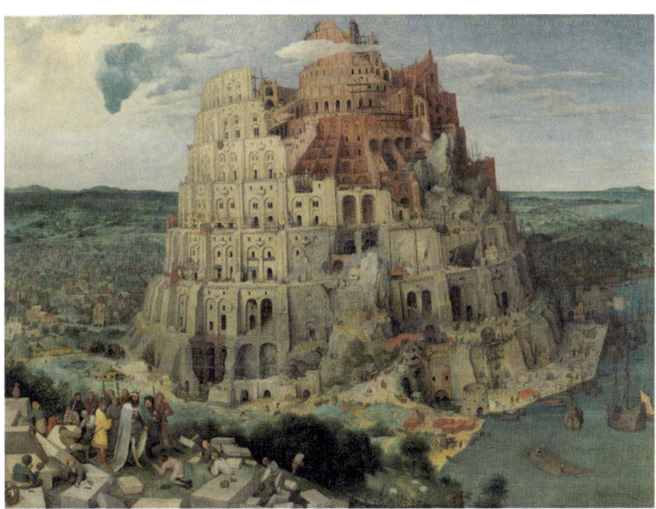

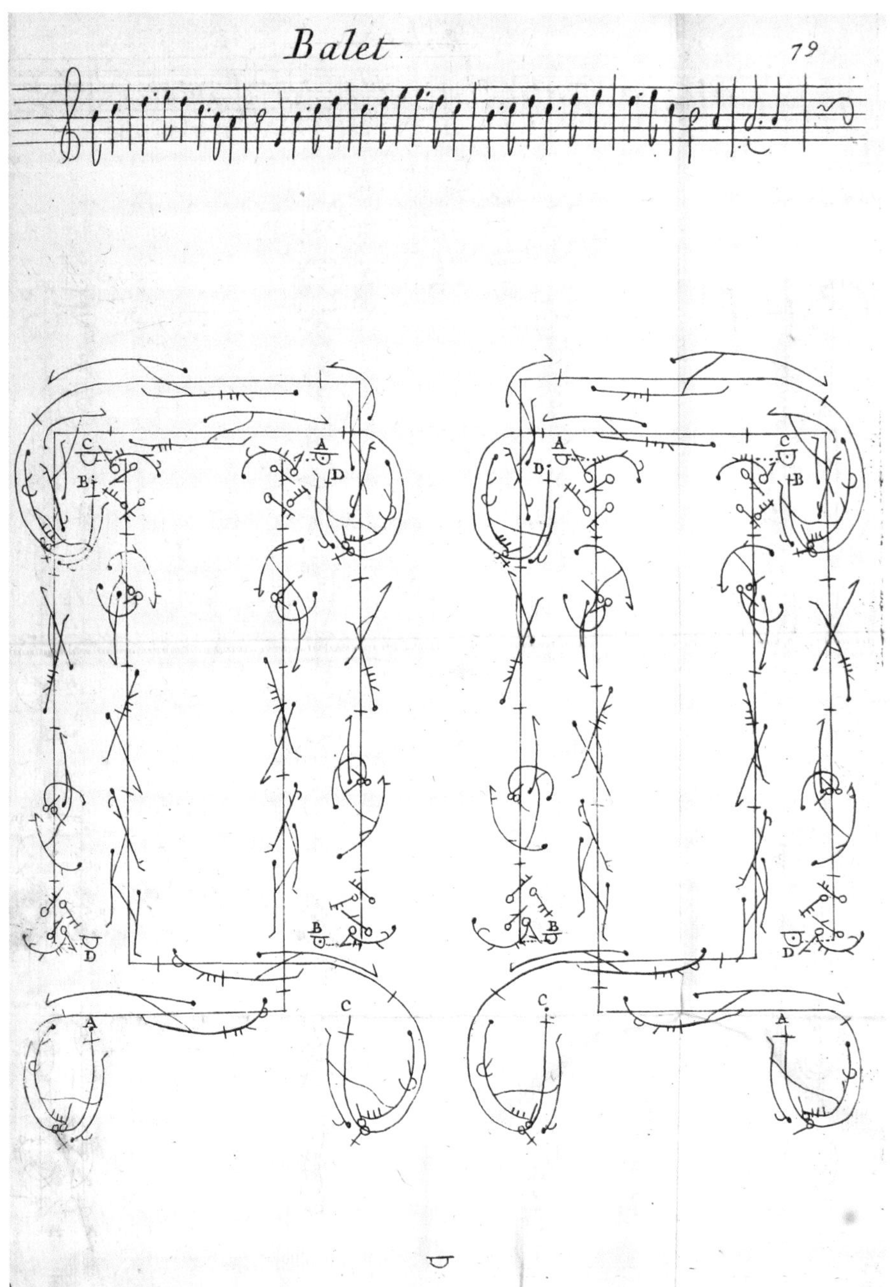

fig. 3   Raoul-Auger Feuillet notation from *Choreographie* (1701).

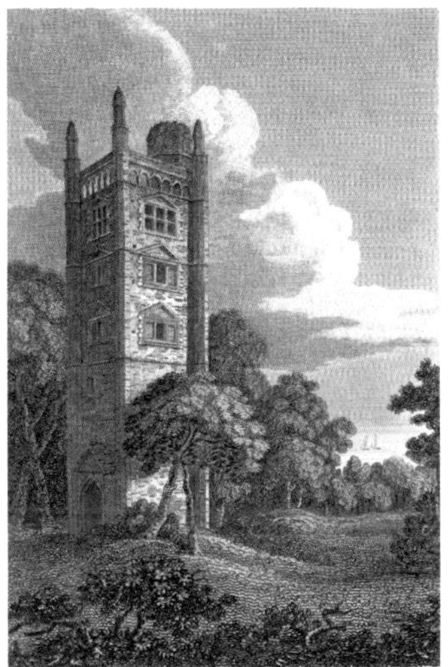

FRESTON TOWER.
near Ipswich
Suffolk.

fig. 4   Engraving of Freston Tower, near
Ipswich, Suffolk, published in 1812.

Pierre Beauchamp invented an early form of dance notation that traced footwork and floor patterns from a bird's-eye view (fig. 3). Beauchamp-Feuillet's notation, which was first published in 1700, resembles less a score for a body in motion than a blueprint for a spindly structure composed of curved lines that crescendo into whorls. Al-Hadid took the irrational leap to make an impossible place. Alone in her studio, she painted the soles of her feet and proceeded to waltz (the lead and the follow parts); her footprints formed a blueprint. Though the artist hadn't set out to build a Gothic cathedral—at the time, she was researching pipe organs—she used wood, polystyrene, plaster, and fiberglass to construct a six-foot-tall example that hewed to the pattern of her solitary footfall. (In the Arab world, she notes, showing the soles of one's feet can indicate disrespect—a cultural implication that soared straight over many Americans' heads when Iraqi journalist Muntadhar al-Zaidi threw his shoes at George W. Bush during a 2008 press conference.[7]) Partly sheathed in a burnt layer evoking cave walls—a nod to mythical grottoes and the geologic formations the artist traversed as a child—Al-Hadid's cathedral is upside-down. Balanced precariously on its spires, it proposes the artist's body as not only implicit in artmaking but also its sacred foundation.

Spatially compressed, temporally scrambled, and consummately ornamental, *Spun of the Limits of my Lonely Waltz* recalls the architectural follies popular in French and English landscape design in the 18th and 19th centuries. Based on Greco-Roman temples, Egyptian pyramids, Gothic towers, or even fantasy architectures in paintings, these scaled-down structures were stubbornly committed to whimsy (hence "folly"), refusing the dictates of functionality and sense-making (fig. 4). In school, Al-Hadid found herself at odds with the principles put forth by Adolf Loos's modernist polemic *Ornament and Crime* (1908), which claimed that ornament (a category into which follies squarely fall) was superfluous, wasteful, and an indication of aesthetic—and even spiritual—inferiority. That text, with its racist overtones, "felt like an assault on my culture," says Al-Hadid, referring to the botanical and calligraphic designs prevalent in Islamic art and architecture. "In my work, I try to give strength to ornamentation: I literally extrude ornament from painting, casting it as a form that stands on its own."[8]

pp. 4–5, 28–31, 43   Consider, for example, her imposing *Smoke Screen* (2015), a 30-foot-long structure that the artist characterizes as "an archway, a

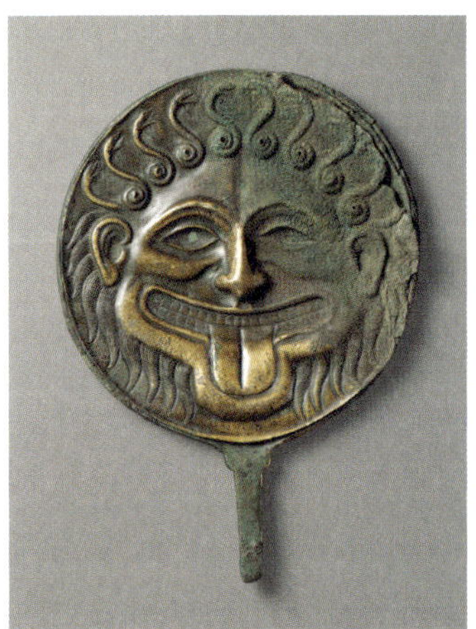

fig. 5   Hand Mirror decorated with the Head of Medusa. Greek, 500–480 BC.

passageway, a dividing wall.["]⁹ On view in *unbecoming*, the filamentary facade presents a scene of figures in a landscape and is topped with gold-leaf flourishes that conjure up the elaborate finials of a Victorian wrought iron gate. The work evokes a history painting that has been burnt, corroded, or cut away—a partial vision of some arcadia. It is, in fact, the result of an additive process, composed from stalactic drips of a pigmented polymer gypsum. To achieve this distinctive visual effect, Al-Hadid paints the industrial composite—prized for its ability to imitate other materials and commonly used in architecture and interior design—directly onto a support such as the walls of her studio, often working off a loose tracing of an art historical reference. Once the composition's pours, puddles, and percolations harden, she pulls off the resultant membrane and gradually reinforces it, as if creating a painting in the round.

The artist describes these works as hovering between fresco and tapestry, media that are frequently associated with decoration or craft and lack a discrete substrate.[10] (Compare paint applied atop canvas with the pigments that fuse with a wall's wet plaster, or the interlocked threads that constitute a weaving.) Though the visual delicacy of the drips makes *Smoke Screen* seem fragile, even wraithlike, the piece is surprisingly sturdy. A smokescreen, after all, is a means to obscure or mislead: a visual diversion, a feint. But what is a smokescreen that declares itself as such from the outset? Al-Hadid's material paradoxes are less barefaced subterfuge than reminders that what we think we see or know is not to be taken at face value. Forms, symbols, and the stories appended to them are not static, but rather slippery, lively, plural, and protean.

pp. 4–5, 28–31, 43

Humans, of course, have a long and violent history of implementing—and then naturalizing—rigid categories and binaries to organize, judge, and "master" the world. What transgresses those boundaries—through excess, leakage, mutability, hybridity, or sheer imagination—is, in turn, cast as monstrous. (Etymologically, "monster" can be traced to the Latin *monere*, "to warn": monsters have been regarded as not only bad omens, but also warnings about the consequences of undesirable behaviors.) As Anne Carson has written, women have historically been viewed as "creature[s] whose boundaries are unstable, whose power to control them is inadequate."[11] The poet-classicist cites such mythological monstresses as Skylla, the Sirens, the Harpies, the Sphinx, and Medusa.

Al-Hadid, that builder of hybrids, has drawn inspiration from Medusa in recent years, making her the subject of works across and between media. "I'm interested in origin stories, in where and how things start," the artist says.[12] There are variants on the myth of how the viper-haired, stony-eyed monstress came to be—for example, in Hesiod's *Theogony* (c. 700 BC), Medusa was born a Gorgon, whereas in Ovid's *Metamorphoses* (8 CE), she was transmogrified as punishment for being raped in Athena's temple. (The boundaries of the story itself, you might say, are unstable.) Medusa met her end when Perseus, regarding her in Athena's mirrored shield, decapitated her; then he took her gaze for his own, turning her head—her power—into a weapon. In a sense, the ancient Greeks followed suit by using the Gorgoneion, an image of Medusa's face, as an apotropaic charm (fig. 5).

In her essay "The Laugh of the Medusa" (1975), Hélène Cixous declared Medusa to be a beautiful woman who laughed in the face of patriarchal narratives and phallogocentrism. This reclamation constituted what the author termed *écriture féminine*: a "volcanic" form of writing, rooted in corporeality, exchange, transformation, and difference, that "brings about an upheaval of the old property crust, carrier of masculine investments."[13] Al-Hadid partakes in the realm of artmaking to volcanic effect.[14‡] The mixed-media wall relief *Blue Medusa* (2023) is a Gorgoneion in which polymer gypsum in oceanic hues forms a coralline mass, foregrounding Medusa's connection to the sea (her parents were sea gods) and coral (which supposedly originated when Perseus put her severed head on a bed of seaweed). A halo of vigorous strokes, energetic as live wires, stands in for Medusa's crowning locks. The gestural abstraction renders it unclear whether we are looking at hair or snakes—which, and whose, Medusa is at play here?

Though *Blue Medusa* is a head-on portrait, there is a gaping lacuna where the Gorgon's face should be. (In contrast, her visage is loosely depicted in *Night Medusa* and *Mad Medusa* [both 2023], works made of linen pulp and cotton on an abaca sheet.) Carson, writing in "The Gender of Sound" (1992), unpacks the longstanding linkage of women's sound to monstrosity and disorder, noting that "putting a door on the female mouth has been an important project of patriarchal culture from antiquity to the present day."[15] She explains that "Gorgon" is derived from the Sanskrit *garg*: "a guttural animal howl that issues as a great wind from the back of the throat through a hugely distended mouth."[16] Perhaps Al-Hadid has removed Medusa's face—emptying

pp. 48, 52–53

pp. 48, 54 | pp. 48, 55

‡
She is in good company: compelling reinterpretations of Medusa's story in art in recent years include Itziar Barrio's *Hydra/Medusa* (2024) and Marianna Simnett's *GORGON* (2023).

the symbol of its content—to relieve the figure of the burden of representation: instead of serving as an object of ideological, narrative, and pedagogical use, she can be open-ended. Or perhaps the hole is a giant mouth, a mouth with no door.

p. 41 Medusa is also the absent subject of *Untitled* (2014–21), a bronze floor sculpture in which a broken hand mirror appears to melt into the ground. The piece is based on a detail from a four-figure classical statue on the façade of the Palais Garnier in Paris. In that sculpture, Jean-Joseph Perraud's *Lyrical Drama* (1865–69) (fig. 6), Medusa steps on the chest of a vanquished man whose face is reflected in a "mirror" held by another figure. An homage to the Gorgon who transformed men into stone, Al-Hadid turned stone into metal to make her version of Perraud's mirror, replicating the form in clay before casting it in wax and then bronze. While Perraud's mirror depicts Medusa's victim, the myth of Perseus features a mirrored shield that reflects Medusa's face, allowing the hero to approach her without being petrified. In Al-Hadid's decontextualized rendition, the false mirror's face is blank as a projection screen, obscuring which version of the myth we are inside. The gesture underscores that as we gaze upon the same objects—in a sense, meet around them—what we elect to see necessarily reflects our own situated, enculturated position. (It's akin to what *Invisible Cities*'s Marco Polo retorted when pressed as to why he wasn't speaking about his home city: "Every time I describe a city I am saying something about Venice."[17])

Reimagining existing stories, structures, and images, Al-Hadid demonstrates the degree to which symbols become untethered from singular meanings or fixed positions, growing unwieldy. This is not only due to the capriciousness of perception—which she highlights in her rigorous formal (material, spatial, scalar) decision-making—but also because symbols are cryptic and contradictory: constantly mutating, multiplying, and merging as they circulate. *unbecoming* may look to historical forms, but it is anticipatory in that anything could become something else soon: we are perpetually on the verge of different possible histories and futures. This is an open-endedness that thrills as it threatens—an embrace of the abiding strangeness of meaning-making. As Al-Hadid wrote in her graduate thesis those years ago: "I want to create a sense of nonsensical logic. In the end, the notion of a proposition is more valuable to me than the proposition itself, the perversion more valuable than the solution."[18] ◆

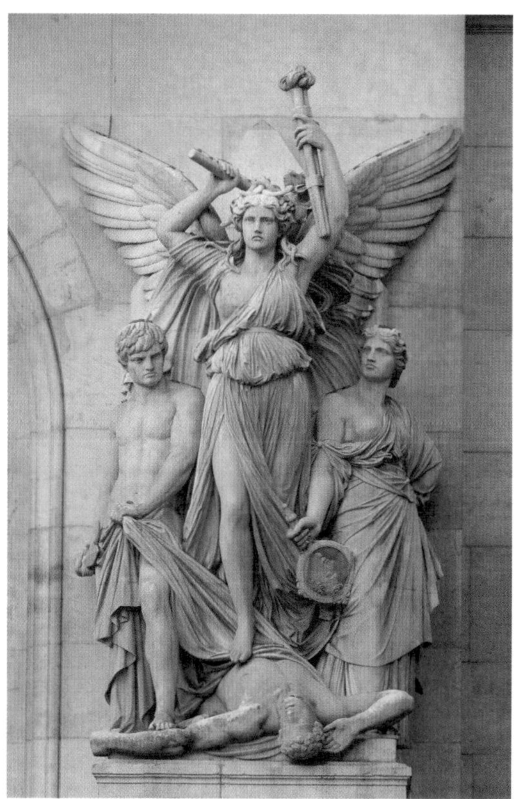

fig. 6 Jean-Joseph Perraud's *Lyrical Drama*, 1865–69, on the façade of the Palais Garnier, Paris.

1. For more on the idea of prose architecture, see: Renee Gladman, *Prose Architectures* (Wave Books, 2017).

2. Italo Calvino, *Invisible Cities* (Harcourt Brace & Company, 1974), 44.

3–5. Diana Al-Hadid in conversation with the author, April 21, 2025.

6. Diana Al-Hadid, "Magic Mountain" (MFA thesis, Virginia Commonwealth University, 2005), 8.

7–8. Diana Al-Hadid in conversation with the author, April 21, 2025.

9. Diana Al-Hadid in conversation with Lucia Simek, "Catching up with Diana Al-Hadid," *The Nasher Magazine* (Spring 2016), nashersculpturecenter.org.

10. Diana Al-Hadid in conversation with the author, April 21, 2025.

11. Anne Carson, "Contempts," *Arion* 16, no. 3 (Winter 2009): 7.

12. Diana Al-Hadid in conversation with the author, April 21, 2025

13. Hélène Cixous, "The Laugh of the Medusa," *Signs* 1, no. 4 (Summer 1976): 888.

14. She is in good company: compelling reinterpretations of Medusa's story in art in recent years include Itziar Barrio's *Hydra/Medusa* (2024) and Marianna Simnett's *GORGON* (2023).

15. Anne Carson, "The Gender of Sound," in *Glass, Irony, and God* (New Directions Books, 1992), 121.

16. Carson, "Gender of Sound," 120.

17. Calvino, *Invisible Cities*, 86.

18. Al-Hadid, "Magic Mountain," 8.

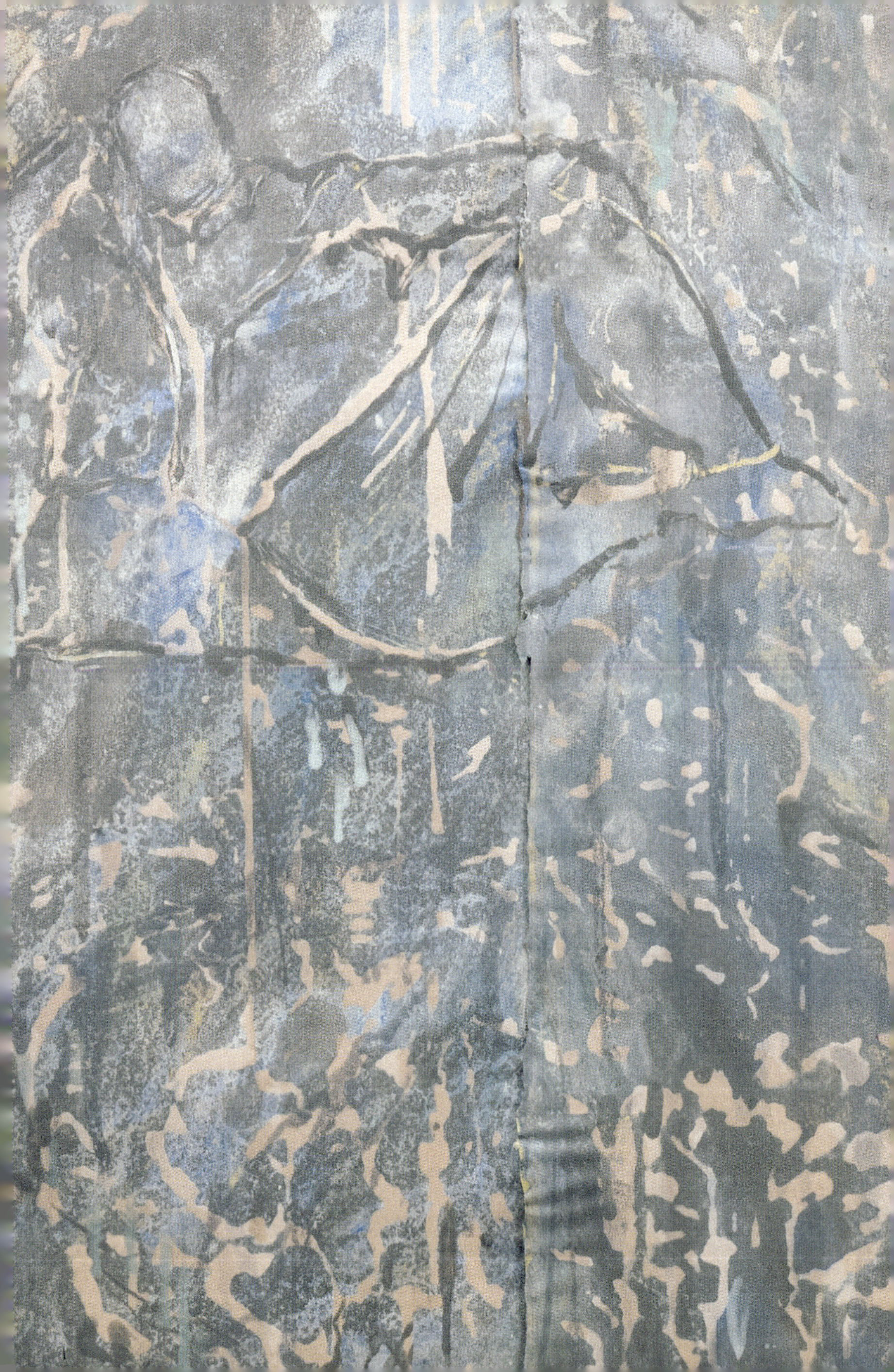

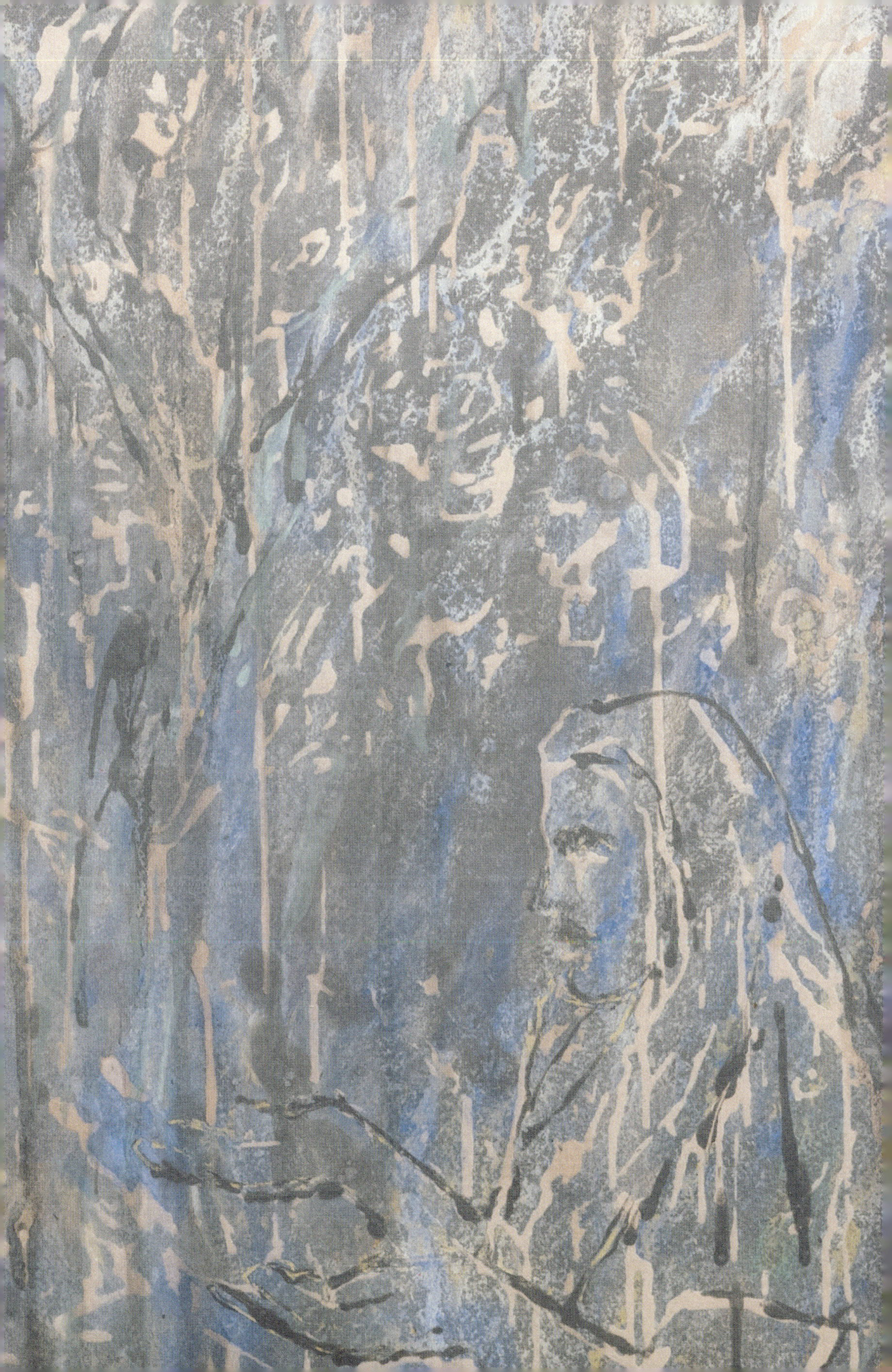

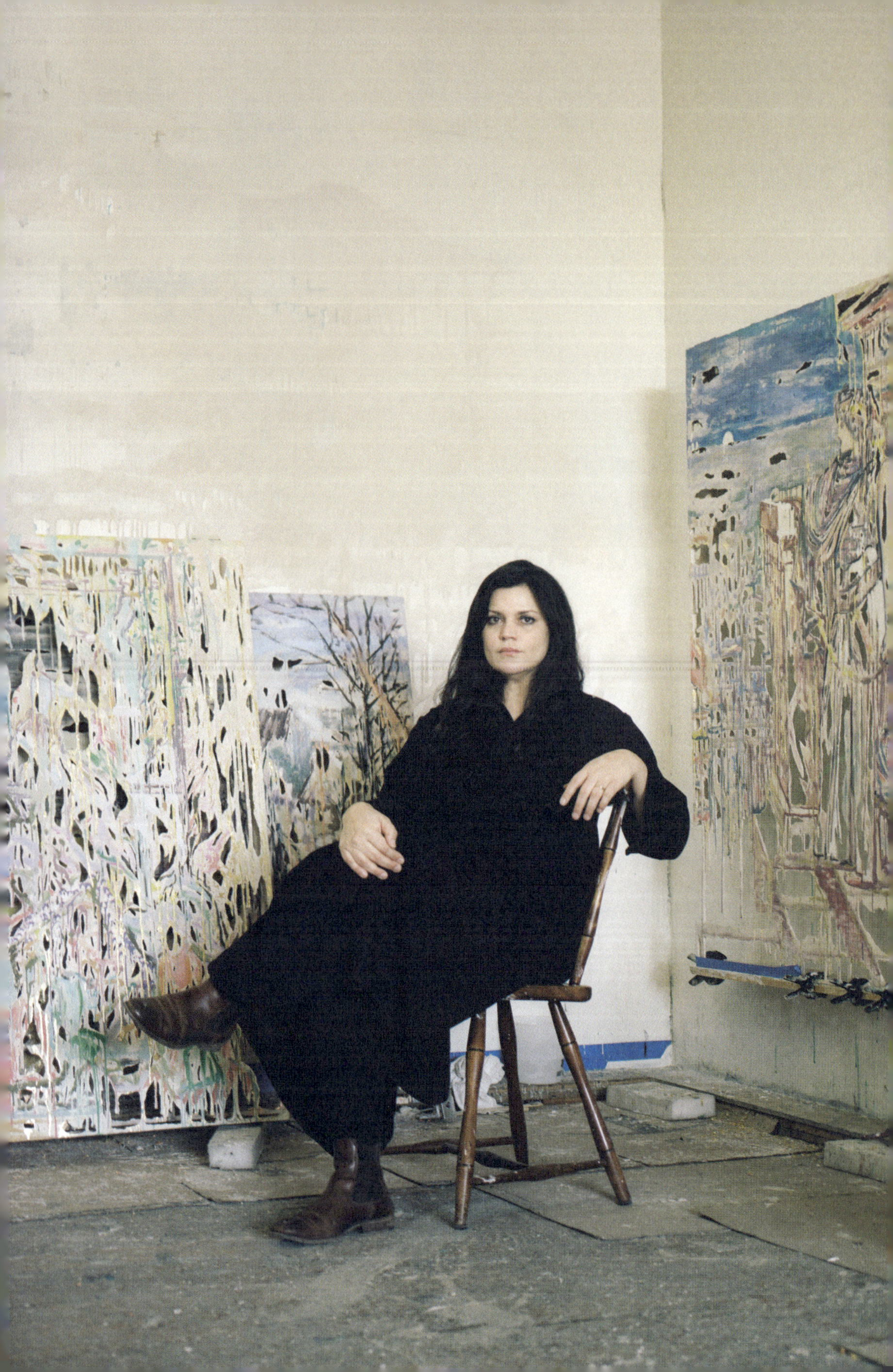

Tracing

Diana Al-Hadid in conversation with Rachel Winter, Ph.D.

March 28, 2025

Rachel Winter How did you become interested in working with handmade paper?

Diana Al-Hadid It was by invitation at first. Dieu Donné came to the studio and we talked about my process and what generates my ideas. Then I went to Dieu Donné and we figured out what the possibilities were with papermaking. The more they would explain different processes and methods, the more excited I would get. It all felt very familiar and inspiring and natural and I couldn't wait to play around.

Thinking back, this is exactly how I came to work with bronze—I was invited by a nonprofit to learn about the process and discover how it can be newly interpreted in my practice. So here's where I give a big shout-out to these artist residencies. The space to play and explore new processes can exponentially open up life-changing new worlds.

How is working with paper similar or different than the accumulative processes of your sculpture or panels? I'm thinking about gestures and marks.

Working with paper felt so natural and familiar because it was very much like the way that I approach image-making in other mediums. It fit somewhere between my works on Mylar ("drawing") and my panels ("painting"). With both, the image is more literally embedded into the surface of the material. They are both built up in layers and made equally in vertical and horizontal orientations, with a lot of pools and drips.

An old friend described my panels as similar to a "cast" painting because it's not actually paint applied onto canvas. It's color embedded *into* the "canvas" (which is not canvas, but a connective membrane nonetheless). And, like paper, both my Mylar and panel works start with a very gestural, drippy picture of something. I start by making washes—basically just throwing around spoonfuls of colored paper pulp onto a wet surface—and it's deliriously fun. I manipulate the material with fine mists, adjusting nozzle pressure and direction; I tilt and prop the board; I use various agents to slow down the drying; I let things settle and rest; and sometimes I mar the surface. I can do different things to thin the layers of paper and build up colors and create beautiful reticulations as the water moves through the clumps of paper.

The grainy trails remind me of the tradition of reading your future with Arabic coffee. After you drink your coffee, you flip the cup upside down so the grinds run down the interior of the cup and create reticulated patterns which a fortune teller interprets. I watched my grandmother's friend read her cup on my first visit back to Syria as a kid and I remember loving the process and the beautiful rivers it created—almost like tiny maps of little worlds.

The papermaking process also really let me freely experiment with color. I've been working with color for so long, obviously, but it really wasn't my first language, so to speak. But I've come to love improvised color play with washes a lot. It's loose and very meditative and I feel I'm in a deep "happy place" flow when I'm pouring colors on a surface and watching them form little geographies.

For most of my life, I have preferred to work on Mylar. For both the paper works and the Mylar works, I start horizontally—building up a color field, a base to build another image over. For the Mylars, I pool washes of colored inks, letting the puddles accumulate over several days. With paper pulp, it felt like a very familiar method of creating a ground, like my Mylar color-pooling phase. But I think with the paper pulp, it's much more forgiving than the ink on Mylar. I can continually thin or thicken the colors with different formulas and make lots of edits to the surface before it is fixed permanently. Then comes the screen over the ground and any retouching after the two planes have been laminated together.

In the past it's been hard for me to draw directly on fiber paper; if I need to erase the image, it may also destroy the paper underneath and I wouldn't have enough paper left to hold an image up. I draw with an eraser as much as I draw with pastels. If I need to erase on Mylar, no problem. And, of course, if I need to edit or restart anything with the paper pulp, that's the easiest thing in the world. I love how flexible and forgiving each process is. How much history of its own making each can hold. How much failure can come before the image is finally set to rest.

Can we think about the idea of the line and the mark beyond the notion of the artistic gesture?

A line can mean so many things—it can be a mark made by human hands, it can suggest a point in time, a fading of time, a trace of something that used to be there. It can also be a boundary, a parameter, create space. This was something I studied closely in grad school; I would often start my sculptures by extruding a line (or a plane) into space. I am obsessed with the idea of boundaries—what they are, where they are, if they exist, how they exist. A line can be so many things.

With the paper pulp screens, I loved the idea that a very faint mark, one that is almost imperceptible, can be cast repeatedly from a pattern. It's similar to silkscreen, but it's technically different than printmaking, as it's more like a physical "cast" of a mark rather than an impression taken from an original. It's subtly more sculptural in that way, I think.

This idea of tracery has always been a big part of my work and my process. I have this kind of compulsion to literally connect to that artist that existed back then, but distorted and reinterpreted in my hand. There is a pleasure in that imperfect translation of something historic. It's intimate and there's a determination to locate a kind of "original" mark. The original mark is mediated first by myself, and then by my assistants who also trace my tracing. Many layers of tracing and imperfect imitation echo forward.

I go back and forth about the idea of tracing and borrowing. I used to wonder how much sampling was theft, but I was also really excited by the idea that I can steal from history, particularly from the Western canon. I can take what I need. That feels like an act of both submission and subversion. Like, I'm going to take just what I need from this, refuse parts of it, and make it mine.

Just how fun it was. After a yearlong residency, I'm still begging for more time at Dieu Donné. I remember it took a few months to really understand the process and the material. I learned about colors and how to slow the drying process, how thin you can get the paper, how the edges of the paper change depending on how you press it. I need to understand a process deeply and fully before I can really use it. I need to know how something is put together, how things work, and what the limitations are. Then I can push against those boundaries and see what new thing there is to explore.

The first thing we tried was a stencil cut of the drippy image I often make when I first begin a work on Mylar. The result was a lovely image, but I thought: *This is the only one I'm going to do like this.* It was a little too fussy and rigid a process, a bit unnatural even if it produced a beautiful image. I decided it would be the only one of its kind and I made it very large. But I knew I wouldn't repeat the process; I needed to work in a way that is more flexible. I like the materials to be agile, forgiving. With all my work, and every process, there's a certain amount of balancing control and chaos.

I also need to be always reacting to something. I think that's why I always start with something that's known—a detail in an image from many years past. I need to start with something; I have a hard time working immediately from a blank page. I need something to respond to, I need a parameter of sorts. Then I can know what the possibilities are and I can make decisions.

I begin by making a drawing on a mosquito netting which we use to make a screen, which we use to blow away paper that's not "cast" from the marks on the screen. This is called a "blowout." The image is built up with almost imperceptibly faint lines, traced until they create a "resist." They are very hard to see, very transparent, thin, and extremely, extremely fine, like old Islamic miniatures or Northern Renaissance paintings, which were often painted with brushes with only two or three hairs. The line work is barely holding onto the screen surface.

I've loved Greek mythology since I was in the seventh grade. I loved all mythological stories. It's why I love *One Thousand and One Nights*. I often get fixated on new stories I've just discovered, so Medusa was a bit out of the norm, as it's such a familiar one. But often these very popular tales have gone through many interpretations, which I find newly interesting. They have big themes that endure and it is compelling to understand why they linger in the popular imagination. Medusa follows the arc of many other mythological or folkloric stories— women who need to be contained and controlled because of the power of their sexuality.

While researching for an upcoming project at Princeton University, I looked through their collection and found these beautiful Medusa mosaics. I was so taken by one particular mosaic of Medusa where she's depicted with this very serene expression. She doesn't look like a scary monster. She has a soft smile and even her snakes were relatively tame. She seemed like a nice, normal person, like the story we know of her fate never really happened to her.

I was thinking about reinterpreting ideas around Medusa's material nature and her liberation. Medusa's strongest material association is rigid and hard; it's stone. I wanted to bring her into the world of liquidity and water, to soften and loosen her up and put her in the context of the sky rather than a dark cave.

Each Medusa work is unique. Even if the screen is repeated, they are a variation of the original. I have complicated feelings about editions, so I made each one a slightly different interpretation, rather than a copy/paste.

I have to give you a lot of credit for this one. I don't remember how we got to talking about Scheherazade or *One Thousand and One Nights*— maybe because I had started to read them to my kid at bedtime? I've made work about her and in her honor in the past, so it's not the first time. But I started thinking: *How do I approach this topic in a way that's not stereotyped or oversimplified or "orientalized"?*

I appreciate the immensity of stories where entire worlds are constructed. Originally, *One Thousand and One Nights* comprises many stories within a story about a woman named Scheherazade. We don't know where exactly the folk stories originated, so I think of the author as Scheherazade, although she is fictional. She introduced the concept of unreliable narrators: You don't know if the person's telling the full story or if they're a little bit crazy. The stories exponentially grow, endlessly unfolding. In fact, I think that the extra "one" in the "one thousand and one" is meant to suggest infinity. It got me thinking about fractal geometry, infinite expansion, and multiple universes. I love Scheherazade as a figure. I love everything she stands for.

To reframe the question: What about the way you approached the visual references in the work?

I went through many different versions of this series, but in the end I conceived of it as two pages in a book, but scaled up to allow for my "drip units."

After thinking about *One Thousand and One Nights* as a collection of folkloric tales, I realized that I had always been more interested in Scheherazade's own story, and the context in which these tales were told, than the tales themselves. So after many failed attempts to picture and render the room in which she, her sister, and the king were seated, I decided I did not want to render them in the reality of the king's bedroom. I wanted to put them in a story of my own imagining, so I placed them within lush, expansive landscapes. I've studied "world landscapes" like Bruegel's *Tower of Babel* for many years, and recently it's found its way back into my life. So I think that was very much on my mind with this series. That painting in particular—*The Tower of Babel*—is funny because it depicts the subject and the context also at odds; Bruegel painted a landscape of his native Belgium in the background of a building of a story from ancient Mesopotamia.

Your brother appears in the series as the king. It's interesting that you're choosing to construct the scene using figures from your own life.

In a way it's pretty simple, as artists will use whatever is immediately in front of them. But I did love having him in my work in a literal and metaphoric sense. I took a picture of Sam when I was home for Thanksgiving recently. My mom's formal guest room has always been very decorated and ornate with a lot of small objects from the Middle East and from travels around the Mediterranean before she immigrated to the States.

There's a lot of ornament, texture, gold, silver, geometric and floral patterns, little glass beads and marble figurines, and, of course, plush furniture. That was the kind of colorful interior design vibe that I grew up with and I loved it. We were not the minimalists of my mother's Western academic artistic counterparts.

Sam was sitting very comfortably in this vibrant context, very kingly and natural-looking. His pose reminded me a little of "the royal ease" pose seen in many Chinese and Indian cultures, with arm extended and balanced over the knee. So I snapped a picture of him and fed it into Photoshop.

On one of our studio visits, you reminded me that Scheherazade's sister Dunyazad was also in the room with her and the king listening to the stories. I couldn't get her presence in the periphery of the stories out of mind... What purpose, what narrative device was she serving? Are we the sister? I guess Sam is the closest thing I have to a sister, but here he sat in the role of a king.

And you are Scheherazade, right?

I guess I am both her and her sister. I took pictures of myself as both the storyteller and the listener and photoshopped them into the image with Sam. I made three combinations of different postures between listener and storyteller and had them sitting in the front, facing each other. The only figure that didn't move was Sam the king.

It was fun to let my "self" back into the narrative. I'm obviously everywhere in my work, in that every mark and decision is mine... But bringing my "self" back into the work literally brought me back to *Spun of the Limits of my Lonely Waltz*, a sculpture I made with my own footprints while dancing. I made it entirely within the parameters of my moving body.

I think there's something really powerful in what you're saying regarding putting yourself in the work. You can extrapolate from that and think about the ways that we're told not to put ourselves in things, to be invisible. If you do see the woman's hand, for example, it is women's work, women's art, or craft. The idea of putting yourself in the work has a much larger significance.

Medusa and Scheherazade are connected to this question of gender, which frames *unbecoming*. Do you have any reflections on what these works mean to you in relation to the exhibition? As your mid-career survey, *unbecoming* returns to questions of gender in a way that is subversive, much like your artistic approach.

Whether it's Gradiva or Medusa, when I work with these figures, these women or characters or storytellers, I want to open them up. I want them to move and be flexible.

As I've said, I love the story of Scheherazade so much. I've always loved this Arab woman who is saving womankind by the force of her creative mind. She and all women are doomed to suffer under this psychopathic kingdom. She intervenes with her art, and her art is what saves her and her sisters. Like what an incredible gift, right? ◆

Detail of *Untitled (Mother Series)*, 2023.

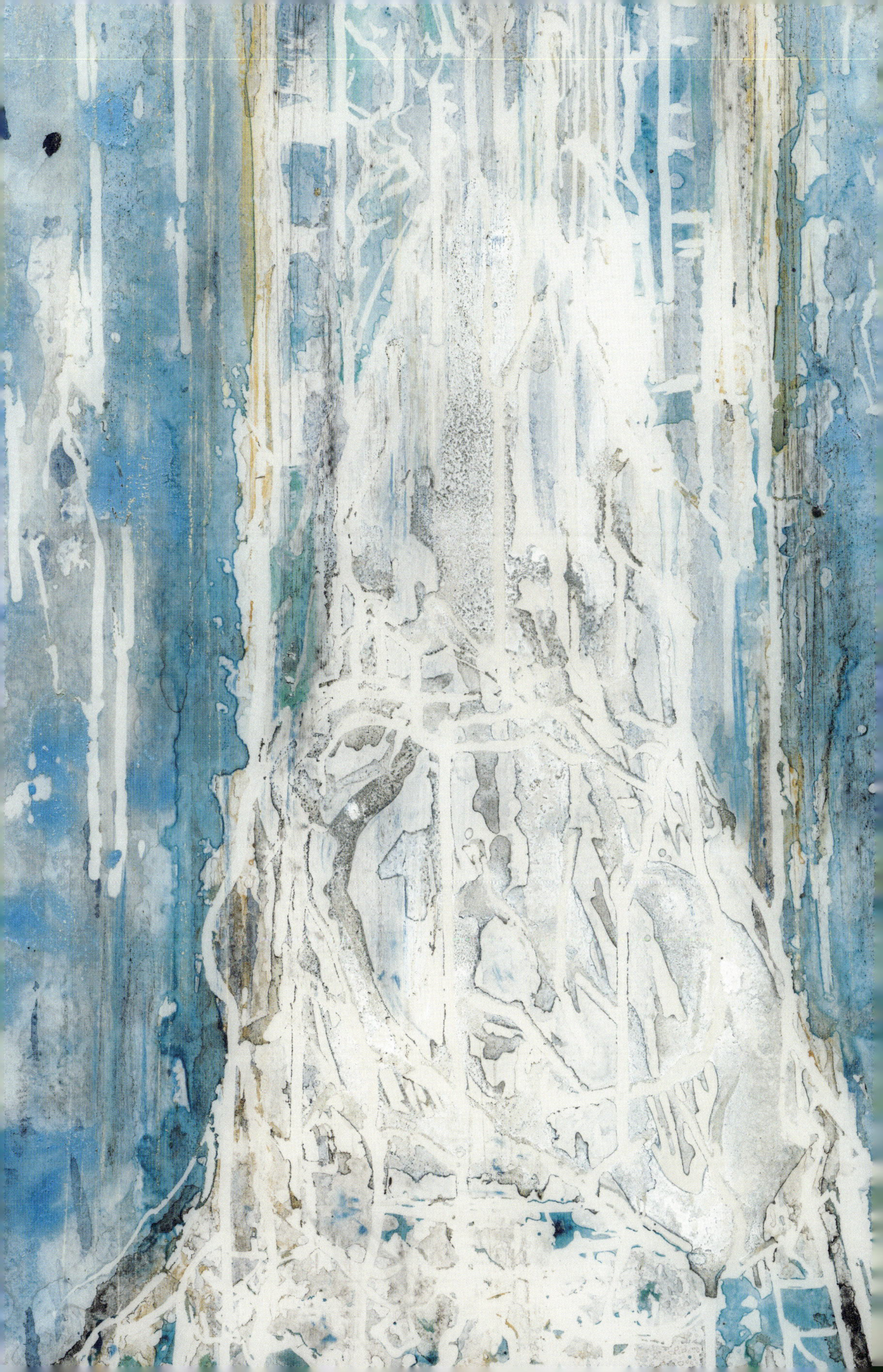

IMAGE CREDITS

Artwork by Diana Al-Hadid © Diana Al-Hadid.
Installation, studio, and artwork photography
by Charlie Rubin and Victoria Loeb, unless
otherwise noted.

BECOMING / UNBECOMING,
BY RACHEL WINTER, PH.D.

fig. 1 Detail of *Spun of the Limits of my Lonely Waltz*,
2006, wood, polystyrene, plaster, fiberglass,
and pigment, 72 x 64 x 64 inches (182.9 x 162.6
x 162.6 cm). Courtesy Morten Viskum Collection.

fig. 2 Diana Al-Hadid's studio after dancing the
waltz in preparation for *Spun of the Limits of my
Lonely Waltz*, 2006. Photo: Courtesy of the artist.

fig. 3 Detail of the mirror in Jean-Joseph Perraud's
Lyrical Drama, 1865–69, on the façade of the Palais
Garnier, Paris. Photo: Marie-Lan Nguyen.

figs. 4–5 Diana Al-Hadid, *The Seventh Month*, 2015,
polymer gypsum, fiberglass, steel, plaster, gold leaf,
and pigment, 109 x 85 x 6 inches (276.9 × 215.9
× 15.2 cm). Toledo Museum of Art, purchased with
funds from the Florence Scott Libbey Bequest in
Memory of her Father, Maurice A. Scott (2017.15).
Photo: Bill Orcutt.

fig. 6 *Gradiva*, originally 5th century CE. Chiaramonti
Museum, Musei Vaticani. Photo: © Governorate of
the Vatican City State–Directorate of the Vatican
Museums.

fig. 7 Hans Memling, *Allegory of Chastity*, 1479–80, oil
on oak panel, 15 1/16 x 12 9/16 inches (38.3 x 31.9 cm).
©Institute of France, Musée Jacquemart-André, Paris
(MJAP-P 857).

fig. 8 Caravaggio, *Head of Medusa*, 1595–98, oil on
canvas mounted on a wood shield, 24 x 22 inches
(60 x 55 cm). Le Gallerie degli Uffizi. Photo:
© Gabinetto Fotografico delle Gallerie degli Uffizi.

fig. 9 Diana Al-Hadid, *Sky Medusa*, 2023, linen pulp
paint and cotton blowout on abaca base sheet,
30 x 40 inches (76.2 x 101.6 cm). Private collection,
courtesy of the artist and Kasmin, New York.

fig. 10 Diana Al-Hadid, *Untitled (Medusa)*, 2023,
conté, charcoal, pastel, and acrylic on Mylar,
19 x 22 inches (48.3 x 55.9 cm). Private collection,
courtesy of the artist and Kasmin, New York.

figs. 11–12 Diana Al-Hadid, *Medusa Rust*, 2023, linen
pulp paint and cotton blowout on abaca base sheet,
30 x 40 inches (76.2 x 101.6 cm). Collection of
Dieu Donné, New York.

fig. 13 Diana Al-Hadid, *Finally, the Emancipation of
Scheherazade*, 2006, fiberglass, vinyl, polystyrene,
plaster, wood, paint, and flock. No longer extant.
Photo: Courtesy of the artist.

EXHIBITION AND PLATES

pp. 4, 13, 29, 30, 32–33 *Spun of the Limits of my Lonely
Waltz*, 2006, wood, polystyrene, plaster, fiberglass,
and pigment, 72 x 64 x 64 inches (182.9 x 162.6 x
162.6 cm). Courtesy Morten Viskum Collection.

pp. 4–5, 28–31, 43 *Smoke Screen*, 2015,
polymer gypsum, fiberglass, steel, gold leaf, plaster,
and pigment, 114 x 360 x variable inches (289.6 x
914.4 x variable cm). Courtesy of the artist and
Kasmin, New York.

pp. 9, 35–37, back cover *August, after The Seventh
Month*, 2025, polymer gypsum, fiberglass, steel,
plaster, metal leaf, and pigment, 109 x 85 x 6 inches
(276.9 x 215.9 x 15.2 cm). Eli and Edythe Broad Art
Museum, Michigan State University, purchase, funded
by the Emma Grace Holmes Endowment, 2025.2.

pp. 36, 39, 91 *Untitled (Mother Series)*, 2023, conté,
charcoal, pastel, and acrylic on Mylar, 22 x 18 inches
(55.9 x 45.7 cm). Courtesy of the artist and Kasmin,
New York.

p. 41 *Untitled*, 2014–21, bronze, 3/4 x 32 x 30 inches
(1.9 x 81.3 x 76.2 cm). Courtesy of the artist and
Kasmin, New York.

pp. 42, 45, **cover** *Mood: 11:14am*, 2024, polymer gypsum, fiberglass, steel, plaster, metal leaf, and pigment, 95 x 74 x 3 inches (241.3 x 188 x 7.6 cm). Courtesy of the artist and Kasmin, New York.

pp. 43, 47 *Mother in the Middle*, 2023, linen pulp paint and cotton blowout on abaca base sheet, 60 1/2 x 40 1/2 inches (153.7 x 102.9 cm). Courtesy of the artist and Kasmin, New York.

pp. 50–51 *Untitled*, 2013, conté, charcoal, pastel, and acrylic on Mylar, 24 x 18 inches (61 x 45.7 cm). Courtesy of the artist.

pp. 48, 52–53 *Blue Medusa*, 2023, mixed media, 84 x 97 x 2 7/8 inches (213.4 x 246.4 x 7.3 cm). Private collection, courtesy of Kasmin, New York.

pp. 48, 54 *Night Medusa*, 2023, linen pulp paint and cotton blowout on abaca base sheet, 30 x 40 inches (76.2 x 101.6 cm). Courtesy of the artist and Kasmin, New York.

pp. 48, 55 *Mad Medusa*, 2023, linen pulp paint and cotton blowout on abaca base sheet, 30 x 40 inches (76.2 x 101.6 cm). Courtesy of the artist and Kasmin, New York.

pp. 24, 48–49, 56, 58–59 *There was and there was not... two sisters who lived in the trees*, 2025, linen pulp paint and cotton blowout on abaca base sheet, 40 x 60 inches (101.6 x 152.4 cm). Created in collaboration with Dieu Donné, New York. Collection of Dieu Donné, New York.

pp. 49, 56–57, 60, 62–63 *There was and there was not... a clever woman in disguise*, 2025, linen pulp paint and cotton blowout on abaca base sheet, 40 x 60 inches (101.6 x 152.4 cm). Created in collaboration with Dieu Donné, New York. Eli and Edythe Broad Art Museum, Michigan State University, donated by the artist and Dieu Donné, New York, 2025.

pp. 49, 57, 61, 82–83 *There was and there was not... a foolish king*, 2025, linen pulp paint and cotton blowout on abaca base sheet, 40 x 60 inches (101.6 x 152.4 cm). Created in collaboration with

Dieu Donné, New York. Courtesy of the artist and Kasmin, New York.

pp. 49, 64, 67 *Lionless*, 2013, polymer gypsum, fiberglass, steel, wood, plaster, and pigment, 64 x 58 x 3 1/4 inches (162.6 x 147.3 x 8.3 cm). Green Family Art Foundation; Courtesy Adam Green Art Advisory. Photo: Pres Rodriguez.

pp. 49, 64–65, 68–69 *Hindsight*, 2020, hand-drawn ballgrain plate lithograph on Essex paper, 39 x 68 inches (99.1 x 172.7 cm), edition of 20, plus 6 artist's proofs. Courtesy of the artist.

pp. 49, 65, 71 *Deluge in the Allegory*, 2020, polymer gypsum, fiberglass, steel, plaster, copper and gold leaf, and pigment, 54 x 42 x 3 1/2 inches (137.2 x 106.7 x 8.9 cm). Courtesy of the artist. Photo: Timothy Doyon.

VARIOUS POSSIBLE HISTORIES BY CASSIE PACKARD

fig. 1 Giovanni Battista Piranesi, *Prima Parte di Architetture, e Prospettive* (*First Edition, Third Issue*), dated 1743 but printed 1747. Courtesy of the National Gallery of Art, Washington, D.C.

fig. 2 Pieter Bruegel the Elder, *The Tower of Babel*, c. 1563. Kunsthistorisches Museum Wien, Gemäldegalerie. © KHM-Museumsverband.

fig. 3 Raoul-Auger Feuillet notation from *Choreographie* (1701).

fig. 4 Engraving of Freston Tower, near Ipswich, Suffolk, published in 1812. Stephen Dorey—Bygone Images / Alamy Stock Photo.

fig. 5 Hand Mirror decorated with the Head of Medusa. Greek, 500–480 BC, bronze. The J. Paul Getty Museum, Villa Collection, Malibu, California, Gift of Barbara and Lawrence Fleischman. Photo: Bruce White Photography.

fig. 6 Jean-Joseph Perraud's *Lyrical Drama*, 1865–69, on the façade of the Palais Garnier, Paris. Photo: Marie-Lan Nguyen.

ACKNOWLEDGMENTS

unbecoming is organized by the Eli and Edythe
Broad Art Museum at Michigan State University and
curated by Rachel Winter, Ph.D., Assistant Curator,
with support from Laine Lord, former Curatorial
Research Assistant. Support for the exhibition is
provided by the Eli and Edythe Broad Endowed
Exhibitions Fund. This publication is made possible
by Lisa Applebaum and April Clobes.

The Eli and Edythe Broad Art Museum extends a
special thank you to Diana Al-Hadid, Kasmin, and
Dieu Donné. Dieu Donné is the leading non-profit
cultural institution dedicated to serving emerging
and established artists through the collaborative
creation of contemporary art using the process of
hand papermaking.

The MSU Broad Art Museum is also grateful
to the Georgetown University Art Galleries, a
presenting venue for *unbecoming*. The presentation
at Georgetown is coordinated by Jaynelle Hazard,
Director & Chief Curator. Special thanks as well
to the Director's Council; Exhibitions Committee;
Emma McMorran, Exhibitions & Public Engagement
Manager; and the exhibitions team at the
Georgetown University Art Galleries for their
support in bringing this important work to the
Washington, D.C. metropolitan region.

Diana would like to thank the teams at Kasmin,
MSU Broad, and Dieu Donné, as well as the
collectors, friends, and writers that made this book
and exhibition possible, including but not limited to:
Eric, Michal, Molly, Emma, Charlie, Rachel, Cassie,
Lisa, April, Amy, Serena, Katelyn, Nathaniel, Jon,
and August.

MSU BROAD ART MUSEUM
EXHIBITIONS TEAM

Installation & Preparation: Jesse Amburgey,
Amy Brown, Brian Kirschensteiner,
Morgan Sego, Steven Stradley, Rachel Vargas
Administration: Steven L. Bridges,
Stephanie Kribs, Rebecca Sun
Communications: Molly Killingbeck,
Chloe Kirchmeier, Zoë Kissel
Development: Liz Ivkovich
Education: Michelle Word
Operations: Dana Steiner

Co-published by the Eli and Edythe Broad Art Museum at Michigan State University and Kasmin Books on the occasion of:

unbecoming

Eli and Edythe Broad Art Museum at Michigan State University
East Lansing, MI
June 7–December 14, 2025

Maria & Alberto de la Cruz Art Gallery, Georgetown University
Art Galleries
Washington, D.C.
January 23–April 12, 2026

Authors: Rachel Winter, Ph.D., Cassie Packard
Editors: Rachel Winter, Ph.D., Molly Taylor
Assistant Editor: Jason Drill
Copy Editor: Sarah Lyn Rogers
Art Direction, Design & Production: Emma Moore
Photography Direction: Charlie Rubin
Photography Assistant: Victoria Loeb

ISBN: 9781947232136
First Printing, edition of 1000

Printed and bound in Italy by Faenza Printing S.p.A.

Distributed by ARTBOOK | D.A.P.
75 Broad Street
Suite 630
New York, NY 10004

Eli and Edythe Broad Art Museum at Michigan State University
547 E Circle Dr.
East Lansing, MI 48824

Kasmin Books
509 West 27th Street
New York, NY 10001

kasmingallery.com | @kasmingallery